100 STARTUPS MADE IN AUSTRIA

EXPLORE THE HIDDEN CHAMPIONS OF THE FUTURE
FROM DEEP TECH SPINOFFS TO DIGITAL CHALLENGERS

BERTHOLD BAUREK-KARLIC
FLORIAN KANDLER

VENIONAIRE
CAPITAL

IMPRINT

100 Startups Made in Austria

ISBN 978-3-200-07223-7
Printed and bound by Neografia, a.s.

PUBLISHER
Home Town Media GmbH, Praterstraße 1, 2nd Floor, Space 21, 1020 Vienna
hometownmedia.eu, office@hometownmedia.eu

EDITORS
Margaret Childs, Ryan Powell

PROOFREADING
Pary Smith

GRAPHIC DESIGN
Karin Dreher, Karin-grafikdesign.com

ICONS
Deopositphotos

AUTHORS
Berthold Baurek-Karlic (Venionaire Capital)
Florian Kandler (Der Perfekte Pitch)
Entries were written by the startups themselves.

PRINTING & BINDING
NEOGRAFIA, a.s., Sučianska 39A
03861 Martin-Priekopa, Slovakia

CONTENTS

INTRODUCTION

HARALD MAHRER

President of the Austrian Federal Economic Chamber (WKÖ).

BUILDING BRIDGES

Austria is a small, open economy in the heart of Europe with close links to both other European Union countries and economies further afield. Export of products and services account for more than 50% of Austrian GDP, so trade and investment make for a "win-win" situation. Some 62,000 Austrian exporters enjoy regular trade links and investment relations with partners in over 200 countries worldwide.

Austria actively encourages its companies to invest abroad, and Austrian businesses have invested €209 billion outside Austria – employing more than one million people in their foreign operations. A new generation of Austrian entrepreneurs sees the whole world as its market, setting up international offices relatively quickly. Austria places particular importance on continuous training for its companies' employees both in and outside Austria, and companies are encouraged to apply the internationally recognised dual system of vocational education and training in their international operations.

ACTIVE IN MULTIPLE SECTORS

According to the Startup Monitor 2019, the IT industry accounts for the largest proportion of Austrian startups, followed by hardware and significant numbers in consumer goods, life sciences and the creative industries.

GOING INTERNATIONAL

Flexibility, technological prowess and diversity are the features of the Austrian startup scene that have seen 74% of Austrian startups enter international markets, with more than 39% of their revenues generated outside Austria.

Austrian entrepreneurs can rely on the support of over 100 Advantage Austria offices worldwide and funds from the go-international initiative, and it is my pleasure to encourage them on their journey of international expansion.

MARGARETE SCHRAMBÖCK

Austrian business manager and politician, currently Austria's Minister of Digital and Economic Affairs and former CEO of A1 Telekom Austria.

RESILIENT ECONOMY

Our economy and the professional world are changing rapidly - in Austria, in Europe, and all around the world. Austria is in a good position thanks to its strong, diversified and export-oriented economy. However, efforts need to be made to identify future industries in which Austria can be an international pioneer A1 in the coming years and decades. Startups play a vital role here. Especially in the current COVID-19 pandemic they have once again proven to be enormously adaptable and innovative. Therefore, it is essential to continuously improve the entrepreneurial environment in order to promote competition, rejuvenate the corporate culture and further innovation.

GLOBAL OUTLOOK

It is our goal to position Austria as a pioneer in innovation. To attain this, we have taken multiple steps in previous years: improved conditions for raising equity, the possibility to found a business online and the expansion of the Global Incubator Network. In addition, via the initiative go-international, we offer multifaceted support to startup founders, including worldwide pitching events, such as startups Go Global aiming to connect entrepreneurs with international investors and venture capitalists. Furthermore, by creating the COVID-19 Startup Aid Fund, we have given Austrian startups which face liquidity concerns easily accessible financial aid.

INNOVATION & PARTICIPATION

Research and innovation is critical for future growth, development and employment. Two thirds of the economic growth in Europe is related to successful research and innovation. Accordingly, we have set incentives such as the creation of a new corporate legal form that offers startups the option of competing internationally and the creation of regulatory sandboxes in which new business models, products and services are tested analytically under official supervision.

We want to be pioneers, not just participants! However, this can only succeed if we sustainably improve current economic structures, further advance Austria's international business standing, implement arising digital opportunities to improve companies and business models and motivate ever more women to found startups.

KEY FACTS

The Austrian Startup Monitor 2019 is the second report about the status, perspectives and ecosystem of startups in Austria. The report is based on a survey of 710 founders and CEOs of Austrian startups conducted in the summer of 2019. In addition, the team used data on all startups that have been identified in Austria since 2008.

Austria has about **1,000 female** and about **4,500 male** startup founders. The number of female founders has increased in the last year, from **12% to 18%.** By now, every third startup has at least one woman in the founding team.

More than **2,200 startups** were founded in Austria in the last ten years. The number of new ventures increased by **15% per year,** which is a much higher growth rate than traditional enterprises which have grown by **3% per year** in the same time period.

14% of all Austrian startups can be considered academic spinoffs, **while 20% were founded** out of existing companies.

The majority of startups is active in the **IT industry,** although the rate has **fallen from 35% in 2018 to 31% in 2019.** Furthermore, there are significant numbers of active startups in **life sciences** and the **creative industries.** Marginal growth can be observed in consumer goods (10% of startups are active in this area) as well as the finance sector (6%).

46% of Austrian startups follow social and/or ecological objectives. Developing sustainable products and services is the most important aim for these companies.

Compared to last year, the average number of employees has increased. On average, a startup employs **9.4 people** (8.2 in 2018). The entire Austrian startup sector now comprises about **17,500** employees.

Nearly 9 out of 10 startups are planning to hire new employees in the next 12, accounting for 40% growth rate from the status quo. An extrapolation based on the total number of Austrian startups indicates that about 7500 new jobs will be created in the coming year.

More than half of all start-ups (52%) have already **acquired external capital** and 63% intend to raise external capital within the next 12 months.

startups' perception of their current hasn't changed significantly since last year. In 2019, more than half of the survey participants perceived the current situation **as good (17%)** or **excellent (35%).**

Only every sixth startup thinks that the Austrian government is seriously interested in supporting startups, a rate which has grown since last year. Among the most important appeals startups would make to policy makers is to decrease income-related social **security payments (44%),** incentives for venture **capital investors (41%)** and higher flexibility and transparency when it comes to **public grant funding (30%).**

More than **90% of all startups** in Austria already generate or plan to generate revenues on international markets. **Every fifth startup is already profitable.**

About half of the startups report to have difficulties acquiring adequate personnel. This is particularly relevant for startups in the growth stage.

Concerning technology and innovation trends, **Artificial Intelligence (67%) is** overwhelmingly considered to be the most important technology of the future. This is followed by **Big Data (38%), Green Tech (32%),** Personalized **Health (29%) and the Internet of Things (28%).**

GO-INTERNATIONAL
HELPS AUSTRIAN STARTUPS SCALE UP

According to the **Austrian Startup Monitor 2019,** more than **2,200 startups** were **founded in Austria** in the last 10 years. Over that time, the number of new ventures increased by **15% per year,** much faster than the 3% growth rate for traditional enterprises in the same period.

TECHNOLOGY AND INNOVATION TRENDS

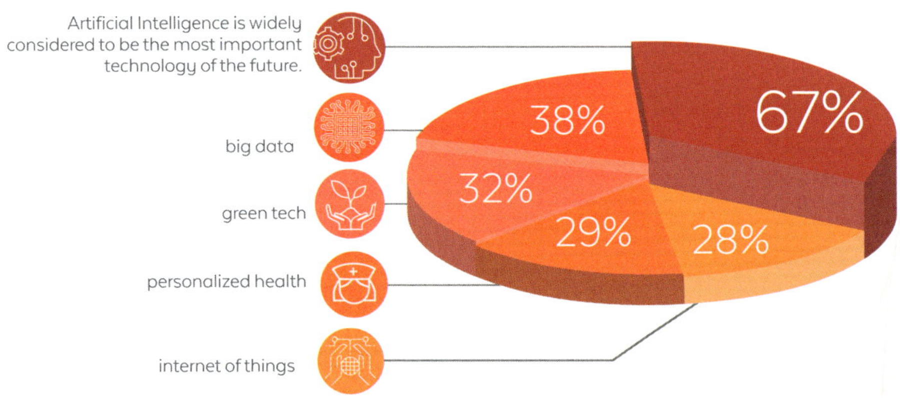

Source: Austria Startup Monitor 2019

More than **90%** of Austrian startups already generate or plan to generate revenue on international markets. Every fifth startup is already profitable.

WHAT IS GO-INTERNATIONAL?

Supporting companies as they grow globally is on the political agenda of most international bodies, including the European Commission and the OECD. A thriving European economy and the global economic outlook make programs like this even more important. Since 2003, Austria has supported companies looking to expand internationally through the go-international program, made possible by the Austrian Federal Ministry for Digital and Economic Affairs and the Austrian Federal Economic Chamber. This program helps Austrian businesses position themselves as reliable partners abroad and equip individual companies with the tools and opportunities to market their products and services internationally. The go-international program is supplemented by direct financial support instruments.

BENEFITS OF GO-INTERNATIONAL

The go-international initiative encourages startups to scale up, aided by Austria's central location and the global mindset of its entrepreneurs.

STARTUPS IN AUSTRIA PROFIT FROM GO-INTERNATIONAL BY...

- receiving direct financial support to meet their targets on international markets
- getting tailored market access coaching from the ADVANTAGE AUSTRIA network
- participating in international technology missions, pitching events, and acceleration programs like GoSiliconValley or Startup Catapult London to find business partners and investors

go international

Federal Ministry
Republic of Austria
Digital and
Economic Affairs

WKO
AUSSENWIRTSCHAFT AUSTRIA

yodel.io

"We started Yodel in 2016. It was clear from the outset that America would be an important market for us, but building business relationships from afar is not easy and opening an office in the valley is prohibitively expensive for a startup. So when we got picked for GoSiliconValley in 2017, the contacts and expertise we picked up in those three months was priceless."

Nina Hödel, Yodel.io

"From a business standpoint, working with partners in the US music industry is invaluable and crucial for Fretello's success. Thanks to go-international, we were able to attend SXSW and the Pitching Days in New York, and went on to secure our first major US partner, Sony/ATV. This was a key moment in our company's success."

Florian Lettner, Fretello

ADVANTAGE AUSTRIA SCALEUPS

Rafael Rasinger, aussenwirtschaft.scaleups@wko.at • +43 590 900-4190
go-international.at/english-summary.html

Vienna
UP'21
Let's talk startups.
26.4. – 12.5.
2021
Join Europe's mos
authentic startup
experience!
viennaUP.co

CONSUMER GOODS & HARDWARE

There are numerous innovative approaches in the consumer goods and hardware market in Austria, ranging from one-of-a-kind snack foods to cutting-edge 3D printers. Nearly 25% of startups in Austria describe their product as belonging to one of these two groups, according to the Austrian Startup Monitor 2019. In the realm of hardware, Austria has a great reputation for efficient supply chains and sustainable production as well as decades of experience in sustainable production plus mechanical and steel engineering.

Alpengummi
DER 1. NATÜRLICHE
KAUGUMMI DER ALPEN
Alpengummi
DER 1. NATÜRLICHE
KAUGUMMI DER ALPEN

ALPENGUMMI

Alpengummi is a gum made with 100% natural and renewable resources

FOUNDED	EXPECTED EXIT	INVESTMENT	HQ	SECTOR	EMPLOYEES
2019	5 YEARS (TRADE/SALE)	0.1 MILLION	VIENNA	FOOD	2

FOUNDER(S)

Claudia Bergero, Sandra Falkner

BIO

Alpengummi is a plastic-free chewing gum based on tree resin and beeswax from Austria.

FOUNDING STORY

We got to know each other during our environmental science studies. In a lecture on forest sector innovation, we were encouraged to write a business plan for a fictitious idea using forest resources. We teamed up and had the idea of creating a new chewing gum based on old traditions. This project eventually turned into the basis for our limited liability company.

We created a natural alternative to conventional, plastic-based chewing gum by first coming across tree resin, which at the time we hardly knew anything about. Then, we found out that tree resin is harvested in Lower Austria in the form of an old handcraft, which is almost extinct nowadays and was declared a UNESCO cultural heritage in 2011. We also realized that regional and natural alternatives to plastic-based chewing gums were missing and that we have a great resource for such a product right on our doorstep. It was clear to us that we had to make this happen!

FINANCING

We financed our business through a mixture of grants, founders' money (and time), and bootstrapping. We have not worked with corporations yet. It is important that the product idea and Intellectual Property (IP) rights are protected and that any cooperation takes place on equal terms. In partnerships, we expect our values will be respected - especially with regard to sustainability - and that there is a willingness to transfer knowledge.

MARKET REACH

Currently, we sell in Austria and Germany and other European countries, mainly via our online shop. In the future, our plan is to explore the Swiss market and expand our sales channels in general. Furthermore, our plan is to sell Alpengummi in the form of goodies and giveaways to companies.

WHY AUSTRIA?

The network of Austrian startups is very beneficial as there are grants available for startups. Our main objective is to create a sustainable and locally manufactured product with short supply chains, so all operations are carried out in Austria. It would be great if founders could receive "founder's income" for the first months because many founders do not earn enough money to sustain themselves in their first years, so we have to live off saved money or have to find investors at early stages. Otherwise, it remains a privilege for some of us use to establish our own company, while others lack the time and money necessary to do so.

LEARNING

If we could start over, we would put more focus on outsourcing production and distribution in order to spend more time on product development, marketing and sales. The greatest challenge was definitely product development. Concerning this, our greatest lesson learned was that the product might never be perfect before launching. However, we would recommend involving other people and gathering feedback where possible to develop the product further.

COVID-19

We focused more on online sales, as we were - like so many others - negatively affected by the shutdown of many retail shops. However, we did not have such a difficult time, as food-based shops were allowed to open again early on. Furthermore, we carried out a crowdfunding campaign during the lockdown, which was risky but, in the end, turned out well.

alpengummi.at

CYBERITH
VIRTUALIZER
ELITE
2

CYBERITH

Professional grade virtual reality treadmills

FOUNDED	EXPECTED EXIT	INVESTMENT	HQ	SECTOR	EMPLOYEES
2014	MERGER, TRADE/SALE, MBO, IPO	1.1 MILLION	ST. PÖLTEN	VIRTUAL REALITY	7

FOUNDER(S)

Tuncay Cakmak, Holger Hager

BIO

Cyberith is an Austrian company founded in 2014 and specialized in locomotion solutions for professional virtual reality applications. This means: Our products allow users to walk and run though infinitely sized virtual reality (VR) environments by actually walking or running. After entering the market in 2016 with our first-generation products, the company introduced its second generation actively powered VR locomotion device in 2019. The motorized Virtualizer Elite 2 uses a 2 DoF Motion Platform to actively support the user's movement, making walking in VR intuitive, easy to learn and physically less effortful.

FOUNDING STORY

We met during our studies at Vienna University of Technology in 2008. In 2012, we developed the first prototype of the Virtualizer, a system that allows people to walk in VR. In 2013, we published our work and exhibited a prototype at several events. The positive response from testimonials motivated us establish Cyberith as a company in 2014.

FINANCING

Starting the company and developing the first product was financed by a mix of founders' sweat, private investors and public grants. Since our first product was launched in 2016, we have been financed by revenues, which we reinvest to improve our products.

MARKET REACH

Cyberith operates globally. We work with a variety of customers ranging from small businesses all the way to multinational corporations and government instituitons. Those who need a professional and well-functioning locomotion solution for VR can typically get a Virtualizer delivered independently to their location. Our goal is to deepen our penetration in the growing markets of business, industrial, and governmental VR applications and to strengthen our competitive edge of providing the best VR locomotion device

WHY AUSTRIA?

We think Austria is a decent country for doing business: It is a state with rule of law in the heart of Europe with full access to the European single market, having properly functioning infrastructure, a fairly well-educated workforce, an industry providing all components required for producing goods, and more. Austria also offers good support for researching companies that is provided by the federal government as well as by the different regions.

LEARNING

While creating a completely new product and building a company, we faced many new challenges and learned a lot. Creating something truly innovative is not easy. There's no role model for which to imitate. We would surely have done many things differently if we were to start over with our current know how.

COVID-19

Many projects came to a halt or were delayed due to COVID-19. Although we are operating in the Virtual Reality industry, our core products are physical products for B2B clients. Independently of specific consumer applications for our Virtualizer, it is typically used at a place where people can come together physically.

cyberith.com

SUPPORTED BY

go international

Federal Ministry Republic of Austria Digital and Economic Affairs

WKO

lifestyle box
lifestyle box
lifestyle box

FREEBIEBOX

A subscription box for fitness, fashion, food and beauty

FOUNDED	EXPECTED EXIT	INVESTMENT	HQ	SECTOR	EMPLOYEES
2018	5 YEARS (TRADE/SALE)	0.17 MILLION	VIENNA	ECOMMERCE	5

FOUNDER(S)

Moritz Lechner, Chris Pollak

BIO

Freebiebox and our Lifestylebox product create surprise boxes sent directly to your homes. The gift boxes are filled with branded products from partner companies. With the help of a questionnaire integrated on our website, we make target-group-specific advertising for our advertising partners on the one hand, and on the other hand, we put together each Freebiebox individually, according to customers and their interests. Products are 70% cheaper than in shops with benefits to firms advertising their products to specific target audiences.

FOUNDING STORY

I started the company originally as a 14-year-old teenager and Chris Pollak later joined first as an intern and then as a co-founder.

FINANCING

We held one funding round with business angels. Technical innovations regarding the delivery processes were crowdfunded.

MARKET REACH

We are focused on Austrian and German markets and plan to expand to other parts of Europe in the coming years.

WHY AUSTRIA?

Austria is a beneficial place to found a company because of its thriving and supportive startup community.

In Austria, we wish there were fewer restrictions and faster processes for founding a company and other bureaucratic necessities.

LEARNING

Looking back on our founding process, we would have proceeded slower and built more efficient processes. We learned that you should always test your products on the market before investing lots of time or money in them.

COVID-19

The effect of the COVID-19 crisis was somewhat negative for our product, since many people began prioritizing savings over purchasing lifestyle products.

lifestylebox.eu

NEOH
FIGHT SUGAR. UNLEASH TASTE.
CrossBar

NEOH

NEOH created a snack that is no longer a guilty pleasure, a chocolate bar with 95% less sugar and 98 calories that tastes better than any other

FOUNDED	EXPECTED EXIT	INVESTMENT	HQ	SECTOR	EMPLOYEES
2016	MBO	2 MILLION	VIENNA	FOOD	13

FOUNDER(S)

Alexander Gänsdorfer (CMO), Adel Hafizovic (CSO), Patrick Kolomaznik (CFO), Manuel Zeller(CEO)

BIO

For 10 years, NEOH has developed and refined a snack that sought to provide an alternative to chocolate products with too much sugar. Our bar has 95% less sugar, and according to market research it tastes even better than many chocolate bars. Our on-the-go product is made with high-fiber ingredients and proteins and has limited impact on a person's blood sugar.

FOUNDING STORY

We want to change the candy shelf of the future to one without sugar. We met at T-Mobile Austria and built a product that we could use for our own purposes.

FINANCING

NEOH is bootstrapped and investor-funded.

MARKET REACH

We currently operate in six countries.

WHY AUSTRIA?

We founded in Austria primarily because it was the homebase for each of our founders. We understand customer behavior in Austria, and since it is relatively small and mangeable, it serves as the perfect market for testing our proof of concept.

We believe that the following changes to the startup community in Austria would improve its success rate: creating a more palatable investment climate with improved conditions to increase the frequency of investment; supporting startups with incidental wage costs; the creation or promotion of state-driven equity programs; and finally, more innovation funding for all varieties of startups, espeicaly those not in the IT sector.

LEARNING

At the end of the day, it is important to realize that founders have to learn every aspect of their startup development. For example, working for a global big player like Deutsche Telekom, you have experts for everything. At a startup, you neither have money nor experts for each task you need accomplished. It is important for startup founders to find innovative ways to learn or accomplish tasks outside of their comfort zone.

COVID-19

COVID-19 did not affect our product directly. However, it should fit well into the post-corona world, especially since diabetes and being overweight have proven to have an effect on the course of infection. In light of this, we have adapted part of our marketing strategy.

neoh.com

“We chose Austria for its access to technical talent ... and its access to grant funding for deep tech companies.”

PRINTSTONES

The leading Austrian manufacturer of individual paving stones and concrete products

FOUNDED	EXPECTED EXIT	INVESTMENT	HQ	SECTOR	EMPLOYEES
2017	6 YEARS (MERGER, TRADE/SALE)	0.18 MILLION	VIENNA	CONSTRUCTION TECH	10

FOUNDER(S)
Herwig Hengl, Keskin Hüseyin

BIO
PrintStones uses concrete-based 3D printing to create logos, emblems and images as paving. With our 3D printing innovation, we can create custom designs and shapes, individual formats and thickness, using wide varieties of color options and service production and installation.

FOUNDING STORY
I brought the team together after struggling to reliably construct pavement structures simulated during my PhD. I found that manually creating pavement structures based on simulations during my PhD in the real world was time-consuming and error prone. To resolve this issue I founded PrintStones, focusing on the automated construction of block pavement.

FINANCING
The company is financed by grants Vienna Business Agency (VBA), the Austrian Research Promotion Agency (FFG), and the Austrian promotional bank (AWS)., and angel investment. We have conducted pilot projects and joint research to evaluate potential applications and use cases.

MARKET REACH
Today we are active in Austria and Germany. Our target markets are in Europe, since equipment can be serviced and shipped more easily, followed by scaling globally later on.

WHY AUSTRIA?
We chose Austria for access to technical talent, cooperation with the Vienna University of Technology (e.g. Material Sciences), and its access to grant funding for deep tech companies. Improvements we would hope for in Austria for startups include a tax-favorable employee stock option program.

LEARNING
Starting over, we would stay focused on the initial idea, avoid distractions and fully master a specific use case before expanding to other product categories. We have learned to establish a core team early and ensure that its interests are aligned, so that staff fully understands the expectations of co-founders and investors.

COVID-19
We did not change our business model due to the impacts of COVID-19, but sales and supply of equipment have been affected. Moreover, production was not possible throughout most of the COVID-19 quarantine since physical presence in the office and workshop was required, yet not possible.

printstones.eu

SUPPORTED BY
go international
Federal Ministry Republic of Austria Digital and Economic Affairs
WKO AUSSENWIRTSCHAFT AUSTRIA

RADICOS TECHNOLOGIES

A powerful fault-tolerant sensor-actuator-network optimized for Industrial IoT applications in harsh environments

FOUNDED	EXPECTED EXIT	INVESTMENT	HQ	SECTOR	EMPLOYEES
2011	2 YEARS (TRADE/SALE)	1.3 MILLION	VIENNA	INDUSTRIAL IOT	4

FOUNDER(S)

Bernhard Heibl, Peter Vockenhuber

BIO

RADICOS is an original equipment manufacturer (OEM) founded to develop, market and globalize TWIN (Two Wire Integrated Network), the world's first integrated digital asset monitoring system and its patented "Computer-in-Cable" Technology,™ which provides roots for Industry 4.0 and Industrial Internet of Things (IoT).

RADICOS technological innovation is a major building block for the Industrial Internet of Things and may be used across a wide range of industry sectors, from oil and gas to maritime and process industries.

FOUNDING STORY

We met at a private dinner party. Two weeks later, we all met and started the project together. Peter understood the Internet of Things and developed monitoring systems 20 years before the term IoT existed. Meanwhile, operators of large industrial assets from different industries and from all over the globe contacted us to realize monitoring solutions for them.

FINANCING

Our company is financed by founder money, public grants and private investors. In our experience, it is quite tough to convince a corporation to share the costs and jointly develop an industry solution. Our cooperations typically start with pilot installations to provide the technical POC for the partner's use case. To date, our partners' engagements varied, from providing the field-test sites and requirements engineering, to covering all costs, or a combination of them.

MARKET REACH

Our business concept is to provide applications for entire industries and to enter into distribution partnerships with leading market players. Depending on the industry application, the markets are national, regional or global.
Our existing partners and continuous negotiations for partnerships are located in the United States, Europe (Germany, Spain, Switzerland, and the United Kingdom), and the Asia-Pacific region (South Korea, India, Indonesia). From next year on, we will be supplying to one of the big tech corporations that distributes globally to the manufacturing industry.

WHY AUSTRIA?

Austria was the right choice due to its high-tech grants programs. However, we wish there was greater availability of significant startup funding options.

LEARNING

From the beginning, we were working in different locations - something we would not do again. After completing our seed phase, we could have focused on a Series A round with international investors earlier.

COVID-19

As provider of a technology for industrial applications, we were hit by the industry lockdown. Nevertheless, we established a supplier partnership with a global tech player during the COVID-19 phase. The partnership will become active next year. Generally, we think that COVID-19 catalyzes the need for higher levels of digitalization of large assets.Hence, we anticipate higher demand for our solution in the mid- and long-term.

radicos.com

RUDY GAMES

Interactive and personalized board games for young gamers

FOUNDED	EXPECTED EXIT	INVESTMENT	HQ	SECTOR	EMPLOYEES
2013	10 YEARS	475,000	LINZ	TOYS AND GAMES	7

FOUNDER(S)
Gertrude Kurzmann, Reinhard Kern, Manfred Lamplmair

BIO
Rudy Games combines the social fun of board games with the multimedia potential of apps, to gets kids and technophile gamers excited about playing board games with family and friends. Content is always up-to-date, personalized and individualized.

FOUNDING STORY
The founders are childhood friends – and the idea spun out of a game night with friends.

FINANCING
Rudy Games is financed by founder capital, government grants and investors.

MARKET REACH
We are currently active in four markets, including Austria, Germany, the United Kingdom and the United States.

WHY AUSTRIA?
It was advantageous to found in Austria because of the high quality of education, infrastructure and availability of government grants.

In our view, Austria could better support the startup ecosystem by facilitating a more versatile investor system that is not so concentrated, and has Series A investor rounds along with other rounds. We also hope that, with time, gaming will be viewed as a serious business.

LEARNING
Our success was acheived by way of mistakes made, and we anticipate this will continue into the future. Over time, we realized how important it is to remain focused, to go to market as soon as possible, to fail often and learn fast.

COVID-19
Due to COVID-19, Rudy Games was able to pivot to online sales through platforms such as Amazon. However, we faced losses at brick-and-mortar retailers who were closed due to COVID-19 regulations.

rudy-games.com

“Focus on building a strong brand and keep improving every day!“

SATURO FOODS

Europe's first complete meal in a bottle - the perfect combination of convenient food and balanced nutrition

FOUNDED	EXPECTED EXIT	INVESTMENT	HQ	SECTOR	EMPLOYEES
2017	3 YEARS (TRADE/SALE)	0.25 MILLION	VIENNA	FOOD AND BEVERAGE	10

FOUNDER(S)

Hannes Feistenauer, Joerg Hauke

BIO

We combine convenience with healthy nutrition and enable sustainable performance. We make complete nutrition effortless and affordable for everybody, anytime. Our customers can choose from ready-to-drink shakes, tasty powder to mix yourself, and a complete bar. Each of our products contains all the nutrients your body needs - be it protein, carbs, vitamins, or minerals.

FOUNDING STORY

Hannes and Joerg met at university. We faced a lack of healthy and convenient food options amid tight study schedules. The available food choices were either unhealthy or expensive, so they took matters into our own hands and decided to create a meal that provides all the nutrients they need.

FINANCING

We bootstrapped at the beginning with the founders' and angel investors' money. Shortly after our launch, we received public backed loans from the Austrian promotional bank to finance our working capital. In 2018, our first big investor, Square One Foods, came on board to finance our expansion. We are currently looking for a new investor to finance further expansion.

MARKET REACH

We are actively selling in all European countries with a focus on the German and English-speaking markets via our online distribution channels. We are very active in the German and Austrian retail market. Our trial period in the United States was also a success and soon, we will expand our market reach even further.

WHY AUSTRIA?

The first producer who believed in the product was Austrian producer. In addition, we built a strong network, especially in Vienna, which made our start fairly easy, so we could focus on the core business right away.

LEARNING

It is not about the big lessons. It is mainly about the small, continuous improvements that make you 1% better every single day. This improves your performance significantly in the long run. It is crucial to build a strong brand especially in the fast-moving consumer goods (FMCG) market. Customers buy your product to a large extent for the feeling your brand gives them. To summarize, focus on building a strong brand and keep improving every day!

COVID-19

COVID-19 has resulted in a positive effect on our business. The willingness to buy food online has increased a lot these days. Customers are looking for food with a long shelf life, in order to be prepared for all eventualities. Saturo is perfect for this while also provides everything your body needs.

saturo.com

SUPPORTED BY

go international

Federal Ministry Republic of Austria Digital and Economic Affairs

WKO

“Every challenge is solvable with a great team, so we have learned to spend a lot of time hiring the right people.”

TIMEULAR

Timeular helps people gain powerful insights into how they spend their time and increase productivty

FOUNDED
2016

EXPECTED EXIT
5 YEARS
(TRADE/SALE, IPO)

INVESTMENT
1.2 MILLION

HQ
VIENNA

SECTOR
PRODUCTIVITY

EMPLOYEES
20

FOUNDER(S)

Manuel Bruschi, Manuel Zoderer

BIO

Our mission is to build the most simple and accurate solution to track, understand and improve the time and value of your activities – giving you the time to explore more valuable things in life.

FOUNDING STORY

We have been friends since we were 15 years old and have gone through high school, university, and many work projects together. We have always been time management nerds, trying to optimize how we spend our time for a more fulfilling and balanced life. Since you cannot improve what you cannot measure, we started by creating an effortless solution to measure your time management.

FINANCING

We started out with our own money, then moved on to crowdfunding, then investors, and along the way had access to grants offered by the Austrian government. We have been part of the SAP.io accelerator and are SAP partners.

MARKET REACH

While we have customers in over 100 countries, we are actively targeting the United States, the United Kingdom and the DACH (Germany, Austria, Switzerland) region. Next comes an expansion across other countries European Union (EU).

WHY AUSTRIA?

Austria was the right choice for many opportunities to get the startup off the ground. We believe that if you want to compete with US or China startups, you need a big market you can operate in with little friction. The EU would be that market, but the bureaucracy required to operate across borders is unbelievable. Austria needs to work with other EU countries on making cross-border operations easier.

LEARNING

Starting over, we would engage more with our users and get better at distilling advice. Every challenge is solvable with a great team, so we have learned to spend a lot of time hiring the right people.

COVID-19

We did not change our strategy and actually observed an increase in demand, due to the increase in people being in charge of their own time management, as workers shifted to remote working. In this environment, our product was highly valued as a tool that helps to improve time management.

timeular.com

TWINGZ

A predictive analytics solution

FOUNDED	EXPECTED EXIT	INVESTMENT	HQ	SECTOR	EMPLOYEES
2011	3-5 YEARS (MERGER, TRADE)	1.8 MILLION	VIENNA	AI & MACHINE LEARNING	19

FOUNDER(S)

Chris Leeb (CVO), Normann Lindner (CDO), Dietmar Millinger (Machine Learning), Patrick Thomas (CTO), Werner Weihs-Sedivy (CEO)

BIO

twingz recognizes activities of appliances and devices by reading meter data feeds from electricity meters and delivers valuable insights to our B2B clients, such as insurance companies and energy companies, which in turn deliver to their client base of SMEs and consumers. The main benefits include fire damage prevention, enabling predictive maintenance and energy-saving.

FOUNDING STORY

The founders met at Startup Live events and via business networks. We started with an internet of things (IoT) platform with digital identities in 2011 and then saw that hardware is not possible without larger investments (which we could not gather). After a market development phase in Amsterdam, we started to focus on applying machine learning in the field of predictive analytics, instead of momentaneous application. The main inspiration for our products and services is client problems and opportunities.

FINANCING

We started twingz by bootstrapping and, after about six months, continued with money from contracts we closed. After that, we held small rounds with Austrian angels, and in 2018 a large angel round of € 1 million. We started to work with corporations in the Netherlands and have stepped back from the direct business-to-consumer approach in late 2015.

MARKET REACH

Currently, twingz is active in Germany, Netherlands, Austria, Switzerland, Slovenia, Belgium, Czechia and in the United Kingdom via partners. Our other priority countries countries are closely bound to the main target areas of our partners Doepke, msg global and FUNK.

WHY AUSTRIA?

Although there are a lot of drawbacks, the main benefits are: valuable research and development support from FFG and AWS in later stages, and staying within your well-known social relationships. The legal situation in Austria is still very cumbersome due to the GmbH structure, while similar structures could provide an easier founding environment for startup companies. The culture of accepting failures is poor - emphasizing the importance of succeeding. The investment climate and volume in Austria is very young - we have Swiss, German, Dutch and US investors in addition to Austrian angels. We think that the tax situation for investments would change this in a major way (e.g. like in the UK).

LEARNING

We would get started with more funding; we experienced a long phase of starvation in the beginning, and after 18 months, our main client announced it would close down business related to our product (renewable energy production) within three months. We were not able to replace what was 80% of turnover at that time. The greatest lesson: Always reserve some time to be able to trust your instincts. The greatest challenge(s): If a major client closes down the business, this is drastic. If oral contracts are not kept or are understood differently in the end, they can be a source of problems.

COVID-19

We experienced negative and positive effects depending on which vertical was using our services. In the industrial sector, new customer projects slowed down. In the insurance and real estate sectors, there was a lot of rearranging - e.g. the latest application of our damage prevention services focuses on consumers' homes instead of office buildings. In remote management of real estate and industrial objects, our applications are highly welcome - the bottleneck is the ability to get data acquisition installed in and around the target objects.

twingz.com

SUPPORTED BY

go international

Federal Ministry Republic of Austria Digital and Economic Affairs

WKO

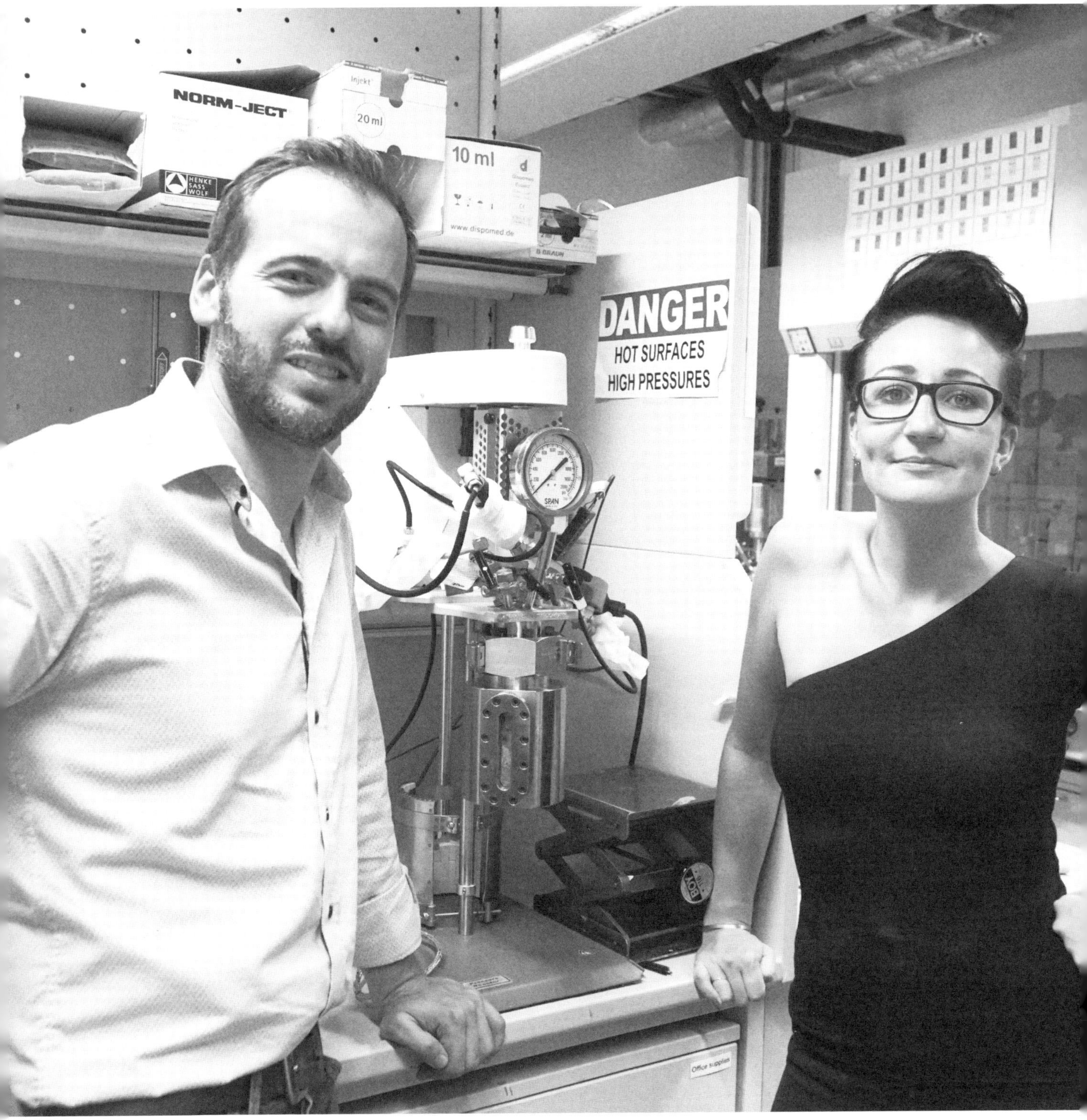
NORM-JECT
HENKE SASS WOLF
20 ml
10 ml
www.dispomed.de
DANGER
HOT SURFACES
HIGH PRESSURES
SPAN
Office supplies

UGP MATERIALS

A hydrothermal process to create unique new polymers, which can be customized to the requirements of clients

FOUNDED	EXPECTED EXIT	INVESTMENT	HQ	SECTOR	EMPLOYEES
2019	MERGER, TRADE/SALE, IPO	275,000	VIENNA	MATERIAL SCIENCE	3

FOUNDER(S)
Dietmar Gombotz, Miriam Unterlass

BIO
The company uses a hydrothermal process to create a unique new polyimide. Those polyimides have unique properties and can be customized to the requirements of the client. Future developments include the creation of other polymers with the hydrothermal process. Our production process allows compliance with the imminent changes in environmental and chemical regulations in the European union markets (REACH).

FOUNDING STORY
The founding team met during a Network Friday of the Innovation Incubation Center. Miriam Unterlass invented the technology at the Vienna Univeristy of Technology and aspired to apply it to real world applications.

FINANCING
At the moment, the company is financed by grants and founders' money. We are pursuing additional Austrian Research Promotion Agency grants and are participating in a set of European grant applications. We are planning our first financing round in the first and second quarters of 2021.

MARKET REACH
We are active in Europe, with a focus on polymer porducers in Austria, Germany and France. Our primary target market is the Japenese plolymer/composite industry.

WHY AUSTRIA?
Our core vision is that we can provide unique products with a short supply chain for European high-tech producers. We chose Austria for its high-skilled labor force, the availability of startup grants and the infrastructure available within Europe. We wish there were easier access to funding and more incentives for the university sector to support spinoffs.

LEARNING
Our unique production process will have a massive impact on the polymer industry, but we found out that working alone, we will not be able to have industry-wide impact. Therefore, we are intensifying our collaboration with industry leaders and niche players in this field. If we could start over, we would be clearer about the path from lab-to-industry, and we would be more strict with suppliers. We have learned that delays in the supply chain have had a massive impact on the successful implementation of our product.

COVID-19
We were negatively affected by the COVID-19 crisis, as a big cooperation project was postponed indefinitely. Current uncertainty and disruptions in supply chains have also pushed back the timeline on other projects.

SUPPORTED BY

go international

Federal Ministry Republic of Austria Digital and Economic Affairs

WKO

ugp-materials.com

UPNANO

Development, production and commercialization of high-resolution 3D printing systems and associated materials

FOUNDED	EXPECTED EXIT	INVESTMENT	HQ	SECTOR	EMPLOYEES
2018	5 YEARS (TRADE/SALE)	0.65 MILLION	VIENNA	ADDITIVE MANUFACTURING	12

FOUNDER(S)

Peter Gruber, Bernhard Küenburg, Denise Mandt, Aleksandr Ovsianikov

BIO

UpNano is a spinoff company of the Vienna University of Technology, developing, manufacturing and marketing high resolution 3D printing systems based on two-photon polymerization and enables new standards in micropart fabrication. Due to the biological background of the research team at university, the system has been developed to also allow biocompatible printing. UpNano aims to become a technology leader in the field of high-resolution 3D printing for both prototyping and industrial applications, providing its customers with comprehensive solutions from a single source.

FOUNDING STORY

The founding team met during their research work and can look back on more than 10 years of experience in the development of high-resolution 3D printing systems . As a spinoff of a very biological research group at the Vienna University of Technology , the original idea was to establish a printing process that allows living cells to be mixed into the material and printed. This approach requires short printing cycles and high printing speeds. With increasing success, the interest in our technology also increased.

FINANCING

The highly innovative approaches of our technology and products has enabled UpNano to take advantage of a wide range of funding opportunities. At the beginning of 2019, we concluded a private investor round to cover the high initial costs and material costs manufacture a demonstration system. In parallel, we work, together with an internationally active medical technology group, on the further development of printing technology and the establishment of new applications.

MARKET REACH

From the beginning, the products were marketed worldwide. The high-resolution 3D printing market is a profitable niche market, so international representation has always been of paramount importance. In addition to a sales manager in the USA, we work globally with selected distributors who support us with local marketing and sales.

WHY AUSTRIA?

Austria offers a wide range of consulting and funding opportunities for young companies and startups. Not all of them seem obvious at first glance, but the startup scene is well connected, and you can easily find help if you want to. We have had very good experience with Austria as a location for startups, and there are many forms of support, for both administrative matters and subsidies. The startup sector in Austria is a constantly growing one, where you can find a lot of exchange and tips and tricks.

LEARNING

After one and a half years, we can say that our ideas and approaches were the right ones. Nevertheless, we would calculate even more capital for the initial development and startup phase, not only to have more leverage for future funding, but also for the serial transition of the machine. When you found a startup, you learn something new almost every day. Above all, the responsibility toward your employees confronts you with new challenges and topics that you have never dealt with before; but also as a person you are developing; you gain experiences that you would not have had as an employee.

COVID-19

The current situation does not leave us unaffected. Given our international clients, we immediately switched to online demonstrations and adapted our marketing materials. Nevertheless, home office, shorter hours in office and investment stoppages have led to delays and postponement of orders.

upnano.at

ELEVATOR

VIEW ELEVATOR

Innovative emergency and sensor-based system for elevators

FOUNDED	EXPECTED EXIT	INVESTMENT	HQ	SECTOR	EMPLOYEES
2014	3 YEARS	1.5 MILLION	FRIEDBURG	SOFTWARE & MECHATRONICS	9

FOUNDER(S)

Johannes Schober

BIO

View Elevator is dedicated to increase lifetime value and safety for all stakeholders with every elevator ride. Our solutions enable integrated sensors in combination with AI to provide solutions for enhanced elevator experience and management, including autoresponsive emergency detection as well as playing content only when people are in the elevator. With viewapp software, we developed a digital management tool for efficient and targeted distribution of media-content to VIEW displays and management of elevator emergency calls. With the latest development VIEW goes beyond emergency calls and is set to disrupt the lifecycle-management of elevators with a producer independent platform, connecting all stakeholders involved in the operation, maintenance and management of elevators.

FOUNDING STORY

We have 30 years of elevator management experience. We built up software competence from the Hagenberg University of Applied Sciences during a research project. With background, in major elevator companies, we created customer-driven products and services.

view-elevator.at

FINANCING

We have been supported by a business angel since the beginning. Overtime, we have received funding from Austrian Research Promotion Agency (FFG), Austrian promotional agency (AWS), the Austrian Federal Economic Chamber (WKO) and the state of Upper Austria. After three years, the Upper Austrian Hightech Fund invested. We have started pilot projects together with KONE, Thyssen and OTIS. We also cooperate with suppliers, elevator management companies and elevator SMEs.

MARKET REACH

We are currently active in the DACH (Germany, Austria, Switzerland) region. In the medium term, we want to work across the EU, due to the ease of market access related to the standardization of legal and normative requirements in the EU.

WHY AUSTRIA?

Through our incubator Tech2b and our investor Upper Austria High Tech Funds, we have great support for founding, growth and contacts. Together with the state of Upper Austria, we have been given access to the public sector. In the Austrian context, we wish for more risk capital, a culture of failure similar to the United States, and one government contact point for startups and funding.

LEARNING

If we started over, we would raise more capital right from the start. However, this is a bit difficult in the EU, as a proof of concept is always required. Working together with corporations was a major challenge. It is difficult here to implement new products and services and bring them to customers. If you want to get into the public sector, you need time and patience, which startups often do not have.

COVID-19

We are constantly developing our products; however, during the COVID-19 crisis, we developed a new platform that will provide better support for elevator operators and we made some adjust-ments to the business model.

SUPPORTED BY
go international
Federal Ministry Republic of Austria Digital and Economic Affairs
WKO

ARTIFICIAL INTELLIGENCE & ROBOTICS

The Austrian artificial intelligence ecosystem is maturing and experiencing further industry specialization. Over 50% of startups in Austria consider machine learning and deep learning as well as intelligent software and decision technology to be a key factor in their software solution. The Austrian AI ecosystem continues to grow by 20% each year, however growth has slowed down slightly in 2020. Robotics, along with AI is a quickly growing sector, which is why Austria has the Austrian Council on Robotics and Artificial Intelligence (ACRAI) to provide human oversight and a clear moral and legal framework for the increasing delegation of decisions to AI systems.

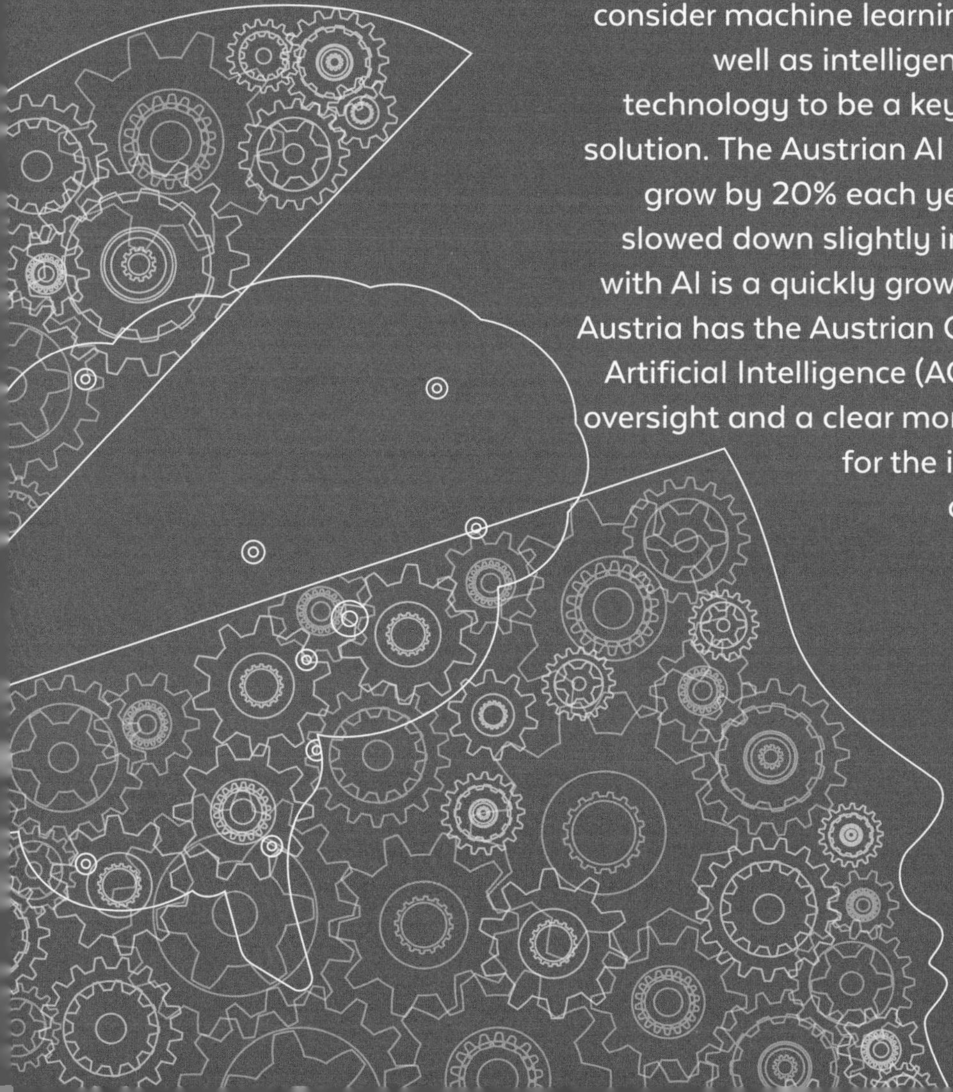

“We learned not to expect things to settle down and stabilize. There is a certain duality to running a growing company.”

ANYLINE

An award-winning mobile text recognition company with the mission to give every device the power to read, interpret, and process visual information

FOUNDED	EXPECTED EXIT	INVESTMENT	HQ	SECTOR	EMPLOYEES
2013	IPO	14.4 MILLION	VIENNA	OCR, AI	80

FOUNDER(S)

Daniel Albertini (CTO), David Dengg (Technical Architect), Jakob Hofer (Business Transformation), Lukas Kinigadner (CEO)

BIO

Anyline provides a toolkit for apps or websites, enabling the scanning and processing of alphanumeric characters. Anyline is fully General Data Protection Regulation (GDPR) compliant and needs no internet connection to process scans.

FOUNDING STORY

The founding team met at the Vienna University of Technology and first formed an ppp development agency, 9Yards. Anyline grew out of a specific project they were working on in their app agency 9Yards for a company called mysugr. We needed a way to make it easier for people with diabetes to record their blood glucose levels, so we developed our first mobile solution to enable diabetics to scan their blood glucose meters with their own cell phone. The moment we saw our mobile scanning solution in action, we knew we had something special.

FINANCING

The company is financed by a combination of grants, bootstrapping and later funding from venture capital groups. The most recent investment was a Series A funding round. We have also partnered with IBM to develop innovative products.

MARKET REACH

Anyline has offices in Austria (Vienna) and the United States (Boston). In addition, we have team members across Europe. Our client base is worldwide.

WHY AUSTRIA?

Vienna attracts a vast pool of well-educated young professionals from around the continent, in particular, from Eastern Europe. This geography, alongside its excellent universities, makes for an ideal location to start and run a business. Vienna is consistently ranked No. 1 worldwide for quality of life, which is a huge pull factor for businesses and employees alike. If you look at the overall venture capital funding and financing opportunities in Vienna, and Austria in general, there is still significant potential for growth. Compared to the UK or other areas like Singapore or the US, it is clear that there is still huge untapped potential for investment.
Austria is one of the richest countries in the world, and while there are some great VC funds, there could be more. Having said that, the funding situation has improved significantly in the past few years, and we're are optimistic it will continue to grow.

LEARNING

If we could start over, we would try more new things quicker. You're capable of more than you think, and starting quickly serves you much better than waiting until you feel you are an "expert."
Making the transition from a startup to a scaleup is a real challenge. It's a good problem to have, but it also means learning and adapting the overall business strategy and professionalizing processes.
We learned not to expect things to settle down and stabilize. There is a certain duality to running a growing company. On the one hand, having clear leadership is vital to ensure everyone is moving in the right direction, but at the same time, it has to stay possible to adapt, sometimes very quickly, and respond to market changes.

COVID-19

As with most companies, 2020 has been a challenging year for Anyline. However, the need for our technology has never been clearer. There is now a large and growing demand for contactless scanning solutions from industries as varied as policing, logistics, health care, retail and logistics, to name just a few. We also offered our technology to frontline services for free to help fight the virus.

anyline.com

SUPPORTED BY
go international
Federal Ministry Republic of Austria Digital and Economic Affairs
WKO

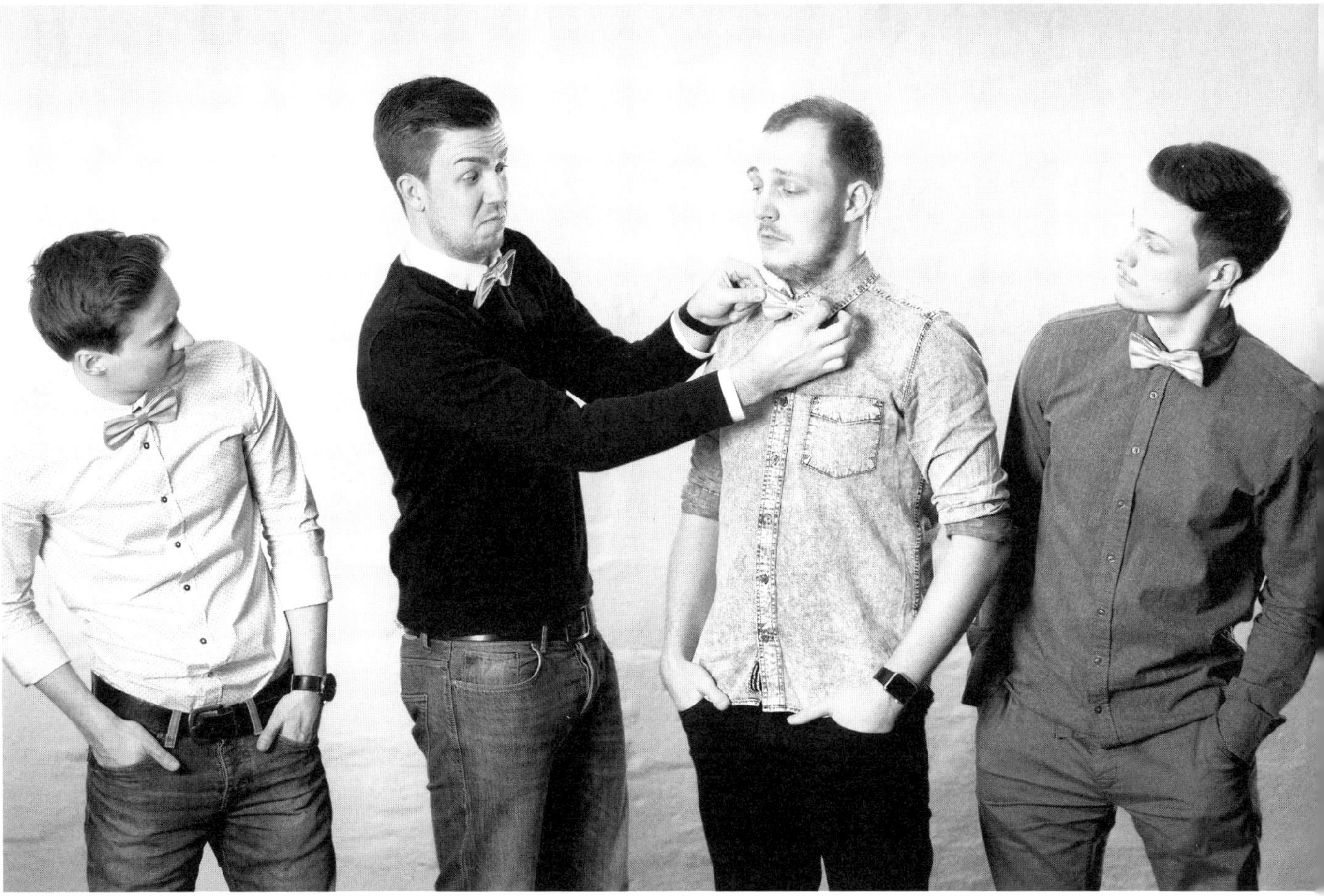

“We learned that in the future we will need to test more aspects of the product and test them earlier.”

BUTLEROY

Artificial intelligence powered and automatically scheduled calendar and to-do list to step up your productivity game and become more organized

FOUNDED	EXPECTED EXIT	INVESTMENT	HQ	SECTOR	EMPLOYEES
2017	4 YEARS (MERGER, TRADE/SALE, MBO)	0.3 MILLION	LINZ	PRODUCTIVITY	5

FOUNDERS

Philipp Baldauf, Philipp Jahoda, Simon Kapl, Gregor Pichler

BIO

Butleroy is an app that works like a personal butler, helping you become more productive and organized by combining and aligning calendar and to-do list.

FOUNDING STORY

The idea was developed while the founders were studying mobile computing at the University of Applied Sciences Hagenberg. Working as freelancers, we noticed how cumbersome it was to coordinate all the different appointments, and we often wished we had a personal butler, so we created one for us and everyone else.

FINANCING

In the first year we survived off founders' money, then received investments and a grant. Besides our main product, Butleroy, we are actively growing our agency business, where we apply our knowledge as startup founders to build great products and companies for corporates.

MARKET REACH

The app is available all over the world; however, we primarily focus our efforts on the DACH region (Germany, Austria, Switzerland) and on the United States.

WHY AUSTRIA?

One benefit of founding a company - especially a tech company - in Austria is that there are a lot of very talented people to hire and work with. This was especially true for us in Linz because of the University of Applied Sciences Hagenberg and the Johannes Kepler University Linz (JKU) right around the corner, where we regularly work with students or research departments.
Austria also provides a great start because of the grants offered for companies in their earlier stages, for everything from expanding their product to other markets or working on an R&D project.
In Austria, we wish for easier and cheaper possibilities to found a company than the current GmbH, which will partly be addressed by the upcoming "Austria Limited." We also believe that something else that would help would be getting rid of the Austrian mindset that failure is bad and that everyone who failed at building a company should never try again. In our opinion, the reality is opposite, since somebody who failed has already learned a lot and is less likely to make the same mistakes again.

LEARNING

We learned that in the future we will need to test more aspects of the product and test them earlier. It is important to receive feedback from the market and a done deal is done only when the ink of the signature has dried: There were multiple occasions in which we had a 100% oral commitment for a project or an investment, and it fell through in the end.

COVID-19

When the COVID-19 crisis started, we noticed that people were more hesitant to download a paid productivity app, so we have been negatively affected, instead increasing engagement in the agency business and in productivity workshops.

butleroy.com

SUPPORTED BY

go international

Federal Ministry Republic of Austria Digital and Economic Affairs

WKO

CRAFTWORKS

Artificial intelligence (AI) and software solutions for predictive quality and maintenance in industrial companies

FOUNDED	EXPECTED EXIT	INVESTMENT	HQ	SECTOR	EMPLOYEES
2014	MBO	N/A	VIENNA	AI	25

FOUNDER(S)
Simon Grabher

BIO
The data generated by industrial and manufacturing plants are used to anticipate failures, react automatically and thus increase efficiency.

FOUNDING STORY
The founding team met at university and while we were collaborating as we worked at different startups. We had seen successful artificial intelligence projects in marketing and wanted to bring this technology to the industrial sector.

FINANCING
The company is mostly bootstrapped but has some public funding. We have partnered with the Austrian machinery manufacturer Springer and founded a joint venture to combine our AI with machines in order to optimize processes in the wood processing industry.

MARKET REACH
We are currently active in five countries (Austria, Germany, Switzerland, Netherlands, and Hungary). We plan to expand to markets in France and Belgium as they also have strong industrial sectors.

WHY AUSTRIA?
Vienna is the city with the best quality of life, and therefore a great place to achieve high employee satisfaction. Austria also offers a variety of public funding options as well as good universities. However, we think it could always be less bureaucratic.

LEARNING
We can say with a clear conscience that there have been no major wrong decisions in recent years. Of course, we would approach one or the other topic differently, but learning and gaining experience are part of life. One of the more important sources of learning was that you should qualify potential clients early on. We wasted too much time running after big names even though they were not interested or had no budget. You should focus on clients who really believe in your team and your product.

COVID-19
During the COVID-19 crisis, we focused even more on saving time within our customers' processes.

craftworks.at

“It’s high time the EU offers an AI with European ethical values.”

LEFTSHIFT ONE

Europe's first independent AI respecting your freedom

FOUNDED	EXPECTED EXIT	INVESTMENT	HQ	SECTOR	EMPLOYEES
2017	5 YEARS (TRADE/SALE, IPO)	2 MILLION	GRAZ	AI	40

FOUNDER(S)

Patrick Ratheiser, Christian Weber

BIO

Leftshift One developed the Artificial Intelligence Operating System – an operating environment for AI. The AI OS functions as both a toolbox for a variety of AI skills, as well as a foundation for creating and running tailor-made AI products. We designed our AI Operating System to be a universal supporter to accompany humans in their daily work routine with maximum flexibility and simple handling.

FOUNDING STORY

When Christian Weber (CTO) sparked the first idea for the innovative AI software that turned into the AI Operating System by Leftshift One, he was already working in the same company as today's CEO, Patrick Ratheiser, and some of the later core team members of Leftshift. After a few months of altering, optimizing and challenging the initial proposal, we decided to fully focus on their revolutionary project, eventually founding Leftshift One in 2017. Seeing how companies such as GAFA misused the data shared with them, the founders realized the immediate need for an ethical alternative. In addition, AI should be made available to everyone in the easiest and most scalable way possible. Technology should always be easy to use and powerful, reliable and trustworthy support to humans.

leftshiftone.com

FINANCING

The company is financed by public grants, founder money, investors, and bootstrapping. Leftshift One already works with several initiatives, clusters and research facilities such as the Know-Center of the University of Technology Graz, AI Austria, Silicon Alps or Green Tech Cluster. In December 2019, the company published the acquisition of an investment by Hermann Hauser and eQventure.

MARKET REACH

Currently, Leftshift One operates in the GSA area looking to quickly expand in these countries. With this momentum, the Austrian high-tech company aims to become the market leader for AI operating systems in Europe.

WHY AUSTRIA?

With American and Asian tech giants dominating the market, it's high time the EU offers an AI with European ethical values. Leftshift One, therefore, focuses on privacy by design, and ethical AI looks promising coming from the center of Europe. With exciting customer fields, high partnership potential and world-class research institutions, Austria is the ideal environment in which to revolutionize the use of AI in a European way.
We think there needs to be way more venture capital available in Austria for risky, yet promising, ideas and we also need to improve failure culture. Making mistakes is part of the learning curve, and taking risks, despite making mistakes, should be encouraged more.

LEARNING

Generally, we are happy about how things have gone, the success we've experienced, and we don't regret our path at all. Though if we really must name one thing we would change, it would be the transition from a project-focused business to a product-focused business. In hindsight, we should have made this move earlier.
As we began growing rapidly, we grew, adapted and expanded our internal structure as well as our routines along with the product, and that was a constant challenge. At first, we didn't expect business development to be as enormously important as it turned out to be. Also, from a founder's perspective, it can be hard to pass on responsibilities for things you always worked on yourself while you were raising your "child."

COVID-19

The situation came with both opportunities and challenges. We needed to adapt and optimize the ways we worked together – figuring out how to best work in a home office situation and still operate as a unit. On the other hand, we were happy to seize the opportunity to focus more on developing the product itself rather than various projects, which helped us make tremendous progress despite difficult times.

SUPPORTED BY

go international

Federal Ministry Republic of Austria Digital and Economic Affairs

WKO AUSSENWIRTSCHAFT AUSTRIA

"We find that all over the world people are impressed by good projects from Austria."

NEWSADOO

Newsadoo changes your consumption of news forever, collecting articles from your most trusted sources and according to your interests

FOUNDED	EXPECTED EXIT	INVESTMENT	HQ	SECTOR	EMPLOYEES
2017	3 YEARS TRADE/SALE, IPO)	3 MILLION	LINZ	AI, MEDIA	13

FOUNDER(S)
David Böhm

BIO
The company developed an app that allows users to read news and articles from all over the world for free on any device, giving publishers an opportunity to make their content accessible to new target groups in a simple and straightforward way.

FOUNDING STORY
Some founders were previously in business together while others were invited later to bring in their knowledge and experience. The idea was spun out of a former business.

FINANCING
Newsadoo was initially financed with founder's capital, then receiving a public grant from the Austrian Research Promotion Agency (FFG), then a business angel, then venture capital, and finally with larger grants from the FFG and the Austrian promotional bank (AWS). We also partner with many large publishers.

MARKET REACH
We are active in the German, Austrian, Switzerland region, in the United Kingdom and Ireland.

WHY AUSTRIA?
Austria is advantageous because it's where the founders come from, it's situated in the middle of Europe, it has innovative universities, and a supportive startup community and government.
In the future, we hope to receive more trust and respect from Austrians. We find that all over the world people are impressed by good projects from Austria, but in Austria there is little belief that a young company from Upper Austria can do something that changes the world.

LEARNING
The primary lesson we learned through founding a company is that having the right team is integral to success.

COVID-19
The crisis had negative and positive effects, leaving our team time for strategic refocusing and improvements in our technology.

newsadoo.com

“We push the limits of sensor technology.”

SENSIDEON

Wireless Heavy-Duty RFID-Sensors for identification and temperature measurement as an enabler of Industrial Internet of Things applications

FOUNDED	EXPECTED EXIT	INVESTMENT	HQ	SECTOR	EMPLOYEES
2014	MERGER, TRADE/SALE, MBO, IPO	N/A	WELS	SMART SENSING	15

FOUNDER(S)

Friedrich Baldinger, René Fachberger, Stefan Fischer

BIO

We digitalize the impossible: As experts in the field of extremely challenging environments, the company develops and sells highly innovative sensor solutions based on wireless communication technologies. The sensors withstand harsh environments like dust, wetness, vibration, high speed and extreme temperatures, and operate without external energy sources. Hence, the passive and analogue measurement principle allows the sensors to be used in various industry segments as for example food, automotive or plant engineering.

FOUNDING STORY

After years of research and development in an explorative environment, we decided to bring our technology to market as we noticed there was an unfulfilled demand for wireless Heavy-Duty RFID-Sensor systems.

FINANCING

The company is financed by investors, the Austrian Research Promotion Agency (FFG), and other grants, and we have continuously worked in partnerships with corporations.

MARKET REACH

Our core market is Central Europe, but demand from other regions and overseas is increasing.

WHY AUSTRIA?

We chose Austria for its stability and skilled workforce. Moreover, Austria has established itself in Europe as a highly qualified driver for automotive developments and innovative mobility concepts. Also, Austria has a very high degree of industrialization, therefore digitalization and wireless sensing are essential for the further development of industrial processes.

LEARNING

If we could start over, we would focus on our minimum viable product (MVP). Our greatest learning has been the experience of scaling up.

COVID-19

During the COVID-19 crisis, we experienced increased diversification. However, the lockdown created various challenges mainly due to an increased uncertainty in one of the company´s core markets – the automotive sector.

sensideon.com

“Our location is attractive because of the world-class reputation of the Austrian industrial sector.”

usePAT

UsePAT improves in-line measurements in various industries to gain real-time accurate data from within the process

FOUNDED
2008

EXPECTED EXIT
N/A

INVESTMENT
300,000

HQ
VIENNA

SECTOR
INDUSTRIAL MEASUREMENTS

EMPLOYEES
9

FOUNDER(S)
Georg Heinz, Stefan Radel

BIO
We offer add-on devices to improve in-line measurements with PAT (Process Analytical Technology) systems. Our products are compatible with a variety of sensors and can be designed and adapted to the specific needs and requirements of many fields of application. Our technology takes advantage of well-controlled ultrasonic fields for spatial particle manipulation in liquids. Based on this, we provide products that have the ability to gather desired particles in specific areas of an ultrasound field, forming a small (but concentrated) transient sample of solids. Users can retrieve real-time data on those agglomerates, which provide a signal similar to sediments, or the de-populated area close by (solid vs. liquid signal).

FOUNDING STORY
The founding team met while studying at the Vienna University of Technology. As the market turned toward data-driven production (industry 4.0) and PAT measurements came into the market, it was time to turn our ideas into practical solutions.

usepat.com

FINANCING
UsePAT is funded by public funds, founders' personal capital, investors and sales. We have partnerships with companies for development and sales.

MARKET REACH
We are represented in six countries, including four in Europe, the United Kingdom and the United States. In the DACH region (Germany, Austria and Switzerland), the density of production in the industrial sector means plenty of business with minimal travel and logistics costs.

WHY AUSTRIA?
It's attractive because of the world-class reputation of the Austrian industrial sector. We had good partners from day one to test our first applications, a good public funding system, valuable private funding, an array of future financing possibilities as well as an abundance of highly skilled and well-educated employees.
If we could change the Austrian startup ecosystem, usePAT would start by creating more efficient industry networks, making more players in the industrial sector available to work in a flexible environment and be willing to take on some risk which should be supported through taxes.

LEARNING
We would have planned more time for development – even though we managed to generate sales in our first year.
Our biggest lesson was that every startup business runs on the people. You have to find the best team members who are willing to go through all stages of the development. Customer-wise, you have to find people who believe in you and your technology.

COVID-19
COVID-19 did not induce any changes to the product, although some projects were postponed. We see a good chance for the crisis having a positive impact, if production comes back to Europe. Furthermore, we are active in pharma – an industry not affected as badly as others by the crisis.

SUPPORTED BY
go international
Federal Ministry Republic of Austria Digital and Economic Affairs
WKO

"We chose Austria for its public subsidies, access to highly skilled talent and research institutions."

WIKITUDE

Shaping the future of cutting-edge augmented reality apps that engage users, add value, cut costs and generate a great ROI

FOUNDED	EXPECTED EXIT	INVESTMENT	HQ	SECTOR	EMPLOYEES
2008	1-3 YEARS (TRADE/SALE)	8 MILLION	SALZBURG	AUGMENTED REALITY	32

FOUNDER(S)
Philipp Breuss-Schneeweiss

BIO
Wikitude is a dynamic augmented reality technology company that provides the tools businesses need to create impactful augmented reality experiences and solutions across industries.

FOUNDING STORY
Our founder built the company as a side project next to his "real job." After an initial funding round, external management joined the team. The idea spun out of research and interactions with the research community.

FINANCING
The company is financed by grants, subsidies and venture capital. Wikitude has significant licensing agreements with large global organizations, including Lenovo, Sony, BP and others. Furthermore, Konica Minolta is an active investor and business partner in the company.

MARKET REACH
We are active globally.

WHY AUSTRIA?
We chose Austria for its public subsidies, access to highly skilled talent, and good relationship with universities and research institutions. However, we wish Austria had less bureaucracy, more incentives for raising additional capital and a better reputation for growing startup companies.

LEARNING
If we could start over, we would focus more on business model and revenue-generating initiatives. We've learned that a deal is not done before the money has hit our bank account.

COVID-19
There was a negative impact in the short run, but we expect to make up for this over the coming months due to increasing overall demand for our products.

wikitude.com

“Our greatest learning has been having to say ‘come back when you are ready’ or ‘no’ if expectations were too far apart.”

X.NEWS INFORMATION TECHNOLOGY

x.news™ is a powerful AI-based live story research tool that monitors sources (news agencies, social media sites, web and internal sources) all in one UI

FOUNDED
2015

EXPECTED EXIT
3 YEARS (MERGER)

INVESTMENT
1.8 MILLION

HQ
PINKAFELD

SECTOR
AI MEDIA

EMPLOYEES
7

FOUNDER(S)

Andreas Pongratz

BIO

x.news information technology is the company behind the award-winning on-demand solution for the modern newsroom and enterprise market, running on various cloud platforms. x.news™ 2.0 even enables the user to search within PDFs, internal IPTC/EXIF image libraries, emails and WhatsApp group chats. With x.news™, journalists can find, follow, collect and share all the latest information to deliver better and faster journalism.

FOUNDING STORY

The founders have known each other since Kindergarten. They eventually founded two companies and decided there was market demand. The idea came from discussions with major international media organizations.

FINANCING

The company is financed by venture capital from family and friends, grants and loans. We have worked with US-based corporations as distribution partners, but not yet with distributors in Austria – integration original equipment manufacturing (OEM) or reselling would all be options to contemplate.

MARKET REACH

Our reach is global, but we want to expand in the USA and become less dependent on indirect channels.

WHY AUSTRIA?

Austria was the best choice for a stable work environment and reasonable costs for developers. Since it attracts international visitors it's a no-brainer for us to invite clients and partners. We hope for reduced taxes and exemptions on taxes and social security costs for the first few years after founding to take the burden off early-stage founders.

LEARNING

If we could start over, we would raise more capital at the beginning to have a longer runway in a global market. Our greatest learning has been having to say "come back when you are ready," or "no" if expectations were too far apart.

COVID-19

During the crisis, we started offering free trials to support our customers working in a home office environment.

x-news.eu

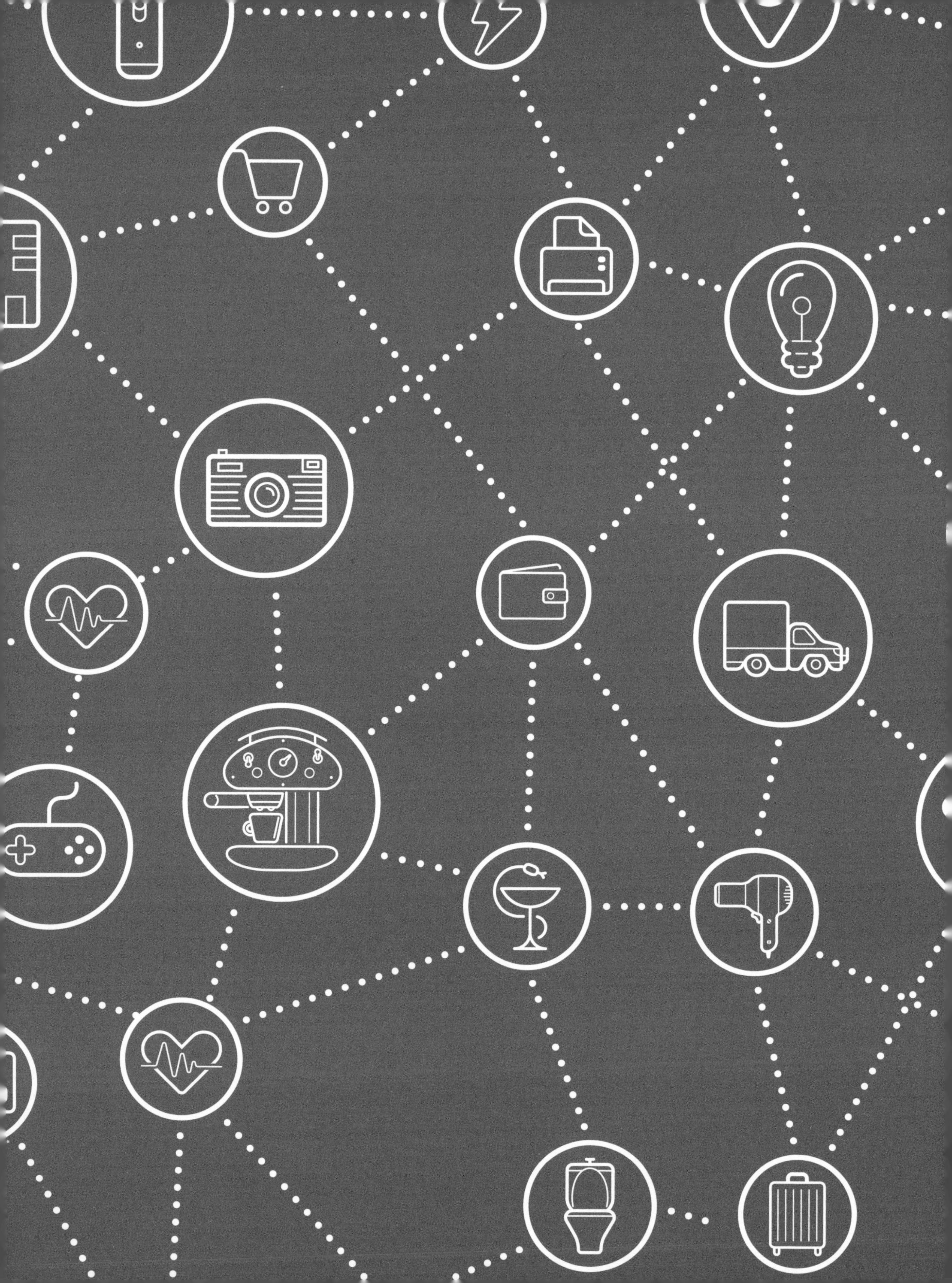

IOT & CLOUD

The Internet of Things (IoT) and cloud startups in Austria power the country's top-of-the-line industrial sector, among other things facilitating better data collection, faster compression and optimized oversights for factories, power plants as well as optimizing storage capacity. The space surrounding cloud services has become increasingly interesting due to security concerns for data storage in the US cloud. Roughly 31.2% of startups categorize their solution as being IoT or cloud-based, according to the Austrian Startup Monitor 2019.

“Starting over, we would be louder and more strategic about raising awareness for each technology milestone and achievement.”

AMLOGY

A leading technology provider for customized and cutting-edge mixed reality solutions

FOUNDED	EXPECTED EXIT	INVESTMENT	HQ	SECTOR	EMPLOYEES
2018	4 YEARS (IPO)	0.4 MILLION	VIENNA	MIXED REALITY	10

FOUNDER(S)

Arkadi Jeghiazaryan (CEO)

BIO

Amlogy focuses on programming content for augmented reality and virtual reality.

FOUNDING STORY

We developed the company as a joint idea to revolutionize the education sector with interactive and easy-access technology.
The idea came from the experience of the founder who had a passion to merge technology with education, and bridge print material with digital content in a sustainable and interactive way. The focus on customizing augmented reality solutions piloted in the education sector and now with the technology completed, we will expand into new sectors.

FINANCING

From 2016 to early 2020, Amlogy was bootstrapped by the founders, coupled with revenue from key projects. In 2020, we received our first round of investor funding, and have also been awarded small government grants.
The company has worked with corporations as partners and clients from the energy sector, retail and government, as well as publishers, hunting and wildlife, and the medical sector.

MARKET REACH

Currently ,we are active in four German-speaking countries. The next target region is Africa, due to the demand for the technology and scalability of the population and market gap.
Another target market is Italy, as augmented reality is still a growing concept. We are als o targeting the Balkans and Eastern Europe due to their early adoption rate of new technology.

WHY AUSTRIA?

Being in Austria gives access to Germany, Austria and Switzerland, all key markets to expand mixed reality technology as it is still in its infancy in these markets and has a high demand and future potential allowing for a first-mover advantage.
That being said, we hope for tax reductions for founders and entrepreneurs' salaries, as well as smoother processes for international recruitment where local talent does not fit the desired profile.

LEARNING

Starting over, we would be louder and more strategic about building awareness for each technology milestone and achievement. We'd also focus on recruiting not only based on skill but on shared values and vision. Our greatest lesson was to invest more time in the recruitment process beyond CVs, but in deeper interviews and implementing a systematic onboarding process. Another lesson was the importance of creating systems and prioritizing time management, especially as the team grew and needed to effectively balance the workflow.

COVID-19

During the COVID-19 crisis, we adapted to better embrace online communication channels to reach our target markets and invested more in online sales through our ecommerce shop. On one hand, we were affected negatively as our clients had halted marketing spending, but on the other hand, we innovated and changed our online sales strategy and are beginning to see the benefits of smart systems in complementing our business model, given that our solutions can already be accessed from anywhere.

amlogy.at

SUPPORTED BY
go international
Federal Ministry Republic of Austria Digital and Economic Affairs
WKO

BITMOVIN

Redefining the viewer experience, while drastically lowering streaming costs

FOUNDED	EXPECTED EXIT	INVESTMENT	HQ	SECTOR	EMPLOYEES
2013	IPO	26.5 MILLION	SAN FRANCISCO	VIDEO STREAMING	158

FOUNDER(S)

Stefan Lederer (CEO), Christopher Mueller (CTO), Christian Timmerer (CIO)

BIO

Bitmovin powers the world's largest OTT online video providers with video developer tools, built by industry experts, using its own encoding, player and analytics products.

FOUNDING STORY

Bitmovin came about as a spin-off from research the founding team did together at the University of Klagenfurt. This is how Stefan Lederer met co-founders Christopher Mueller and Christian Timmerer, who was Lederer's professor at that time. During their PhDs, they co-created the MPEG-DASH video streaming standard, which is used by YouTube, Netflix, Hulu, etc. today, and which is used in total for more than 50% of the peak internet traffic. The research evolved into the company, with the help of angel investors including senior people at Cisco, Netflix, Accenture, Drupal and DropBox. Bitmovin is about solving complex problems in engineering and, in particular video. Based on this expertise, traction and success, we wanted to build the most efficient video infrastructure products, and that led us to start Bitmovin.

FINANCING

The company is financed through investors, including Y Combinator, Atomico, Highland Europe, Speedinvest, Dawn Capital and Constantia.
We have a wide range of strong technology partners that have helped us in our growth, such as Amazon Web Services, Google Cloud, Microsoft, Irdeto, etc.

MARKET REACH

We already operate globally with a strong focus on the American market followed by Europe, the Middle East and Africa (EMEA) and Asia-Pacific (APAC), since streaming has become a global phenomenon. We're excited to already be working with so many customers worldwide. Customers in the United States include Znipe.TV, The New York Times, Classpass and others. In EMEA, they include the BBC, Red Bull Media, RTL, ProsiebenSat1 and more. In APAC, initial customers include Iflix.

WHY AUSTRIA?

Founding in Austria has benefitted us in several ways, particularly giving us access to great international talent and the high-quality output of universities in the country.

LEARNING

If the founder could start over, he would try to gain more experience that would help him along the way. As a first-time founder, you learn so much on the way, but it is better to have experience before you start. The greatest challenge was learning how to transform a technology to a product with a go-to-market strategy.

COVID-19

COVID-19 did not stop us from innovating throughout the entire company. We switched, for example, to more digital marketing initiatives, such as virtual events, in order to reach our customers and target audience and learned from their data. We quickly saw that video usage increased but also that many sport events got negatively affected. This has, right now, only a neutral effect on us, but potentially a very positive one in the long term.

bitmovin.com

SUPPORTED BY
go international
Federal Ministry
Republic of Austria
Digital and
Economic Affairs
WKO

“As for many startups, selling successfully and growing sales quickly (by 100%/year) is the biggest challenge.”

CRATE.IO

Helping businesses use their data, by developing technologies that combine real-time performance with the ease of SQL

FOUNDED	EXPECTED EXIT	INVESTMENT	HQ	SECTOR	EMPLOYEES
2013	3 YEARS (TRADE/SALE, IPO)	23 MILLION	SAN FRANCISCO, DORNBIRN	DATA/IOT	68

FOUNDER(S)

Bernd Dorn (CTO), Christian Lutz (President), Eva Schönleitner (CEO)

BIO

CrateDB is an industrial-grade database cleverly extending the limits of traditional time-series databases. Large-scale machine data poses challenges other time-series databases cannot meet – the need to scale volume and variety while running aggregated complex real-time queries, with high availability and velocity anywhere. All without driving up costs and keeping familiar SQL interface.

FOUNDING STORY

Jodok Batlogg and Bernd Dorn worked together on the large scale web platform StudiVZ, where the idea for Crate emerged. A new kind of distributed SQL database was born to deal with the ever growing demand in data management, especially having IoT/IIoT and time series in mind. Christian Lutz had already executed three successful VC funded startups and exits, and joined the team to help fundraise. All together we founded Crate in 2013 which then got VC-funded. In 2020 founders and board decided to grow the company with a new CEO Eva, where Christian took the role of president. In Oct 2019 Bernd took over the CTO role from Jodok.

FINANCING

Crate is a venture capital backed company, with investors from San Francisco, London, Munich, Vienna and more. Crate leveraged research and development debt-grant-funding from FFG and Investitionsbank Berlin (IBB). In addition, some of our customers have invested along the way. Crate is planning an expansionary fundraising round for 2021.

MARKET REACH

Our main customers are in Austria, Germany, Switzerland and the US. There is a lot of room to expand in these markets and into more EU countries, before we plan to approach Asia. Due to COVID-19 measures, we will focus on Germany, Austria and Switzerland.

WHY AUSTRIA?

This region is advantageous for its highly capabilty manufacturing, industrial IoT and the availability of advanced data analytics. We wanted to launch the company where we wanted to live and leverage our local networks of friends and businesses. The region around Lake Constance has lots of great companies and people. In addition, we have offices in Berlin and San Francisco for those who love cities. To improve growth of Austrian startups, the tax regime for options, valuations and for investors should be reformed. The reality of doing business for startups is not compatible with old rules and thinking. This references the valuation gains and losses within a fiscal year. These can be huge. High valuations can get taxed despite them having no cash effect in reality, which creates huge problems and disadvantages.

LEARNING

If we could start over, we would go to market sooner to get feedback early, be much more focused on sales and raise much more money in the beginning. Getting our sales strategy right has been the most difficult problem to master. Also, the dynamics of growing from a small family-and-friends oriented startup into a growth company with different style has proven to be a challenge and requires that team and founders have to transition. We have learned that nothing is set in stone. As is the case for many, selling successfully and growing sales quickly (by at least 100%/year) is the biggest challenge.

COVID-19

In response to the COVID-19 crisis, we evolved our sales and marketing capabilities, with less focus on the product. We felt some negative impact in our Q1 and Q2 2020 sales, but also positive effects as numbers of customers is growing. Overall we could close a funding round in Q4 2020 and are now aggressively building out our sales for 2021.

SUPPORTED BY

go international

Federal Ministry Republic of Austria Digital and Economic Affairs

WKO

crate.io

“The advantage of being small is being open to opportunities and being flexible enough to take them.”

EASYSOLUTIONS

The platform for a connected world to manage and monitor all internet and telephone services with the power of an ACS

FOUNDED	EXPECTED EXIT	INVESTMENT	HQ	SECTOR	EMPLOYEES
2017	MERGER, MBO, IPO	N/A	WENDLING	TELECOMMUNI-CATIONS, ISPS	4

FOUNDER(S)

Christian Aichinger, Mathias Aichinger, Robert Wurm

BIO

EasySolutions is a software company and its expertise includes techniques of modern software engineering and network technology. The company specializes in the development of enterprise applications for internet service providers allowing network operators to manage and analyze terminal devices.

FOUNDING STORY

Christian had a company with an outdated product. When new requirements popped up – and since he was not a developer – he needed to decide between buying an existing solution from a competitor or hiring people to develop a new solution. Fortunately, his son was studying software engineering and was open to the idea. He also asked his classmate Robert to join the team and together they founded EasySolutions GmbH.

FINANCING

Our company is completely bootstrapped. Existing customers from the sister company have helped to keep cashflow positive from the beginning. We do not see the need for investors at the moment, but are open for cooperating with partners.

MARKET REACH

Having already sold our product to companies in seven European countries, we want to increase sales in Europe, but are also looking at markets on other continents.

WHY AUSTRIA?

We think that Austria is a beautiful country with a good economy, but we wish for less bureaucracy and more stress on education in the digital industries and for development courses in schools, which would be a great step in getting more people into digital industries.

LEARNING

We have learned that the biggest advantage of being small (as opposed to being big players in the market) is being open to new opportunities and being flexible enough to take them.

COVID-19

The COVID-19 crisis has been the best advertisement for our customers (internet service providers). Quite suddenly, governments have recognized the internet as critical infrastructure. This positive uptick in the sector triggered customers to invest even more into their infrastructure, and we have had more projects than usual.

easysol.at

“The next countries we will expand to are Finland, Spain, Italy, France and the CEE Region, not necessarily in that order.”

HYDROGRID

An automated IoT software for optimal, real-time planning and dispatch of hydropower plants

FOUNDED	EXPECTED EXIT	INVESTMENT	HQ	SECTOR	EMPLOYEES
2016	4 YEARS (TRADE/SALE, IPO)	€3.2 MILLION	VIENNA	ENERGY	15

FOUNDER(S)

Janice Goodenough

BIO

The all-in-one Software-as-a-Service (SaaS) solution for daily optimal hydropower management and dispatch. Our 365-days-a-year optimal production planning & dispatch SaaS solution enables power plant owners to increase their revenues by up to 18% by aligning their production to the power markets while at the same time reducing daily operational workload.

FOUNDING STORY

Janice Goodenough founded the company in 2016 and immediately hired Kiran Madisetti, former CEO of EnerjiSa, one of Turkey's largest power trading companies. The leadership team expanded to include Andreas Lichtl (CFO) and Annette Mossel (COO) who each bring their individual expertise to Hydrogrid. Janice Goodenough spent eight years acquiring first-hand knowledge of the issues hydropower plant operators face while leading the quantitative analytics team for Austria's largest hydro power producer. She identified a market gap for a cost-effective solution for small/mid-sized hydropower plant operators and founded Hydrogrid.

FINANCING

Hydrogrid initially raised capital from three business angels. Since then, Hydrogrid has also attracted an institutional investor in its late seed round and received various innovation grants, totaling more than €3 million in funding by June 2020. Hydrogrid works with multiple corporations as partners and most recently as a late seed investor. Hydrogrid is currently in talks with corporate partners who may support it in scaling the business more rapidly.

MARKET REACH

Currently, Hydrogrid is active in five countries: Norway, UK, Sweden, Turkey and Bosnia. Hydropower is a prevalent source of energy in Europe, so we are not limited to any specific country. Countries we will expand to are Finland, Spain, Italy, France and the Centeral and Eastern Europe (CEE) Region, not necessarily in that order. Our market research yields favorable circumstances in terms of pain points of local customers and modernization of the hydropower infrastructure.

WHY AUSTRIA?

Austria, particularly Vienna, is a great location to start a company. The availability of federal grants and early investment opportunities is one of the best in Europe. Employers can also draw from a pool of highly skilled professionals across the EU. Nonetheless, improvements would include lower wage taxes, less bureaucracy when hiring professionals from outside the EU - getting an Red-White-Red Card card is a huge hassle - and better infrastructure for later stage investments (Series A onward). A tax-friendly way of handling VSOP programs (similar to US) would be great.

LEARNING

Hindsight is always 20/20, but when it comes down to it, founding a startup is all about learning to overcome new challenges. One thing we would do differently would be to focus heavily on marketing and sales from the very first day, rather than first building an amazing product - many tech founders are guilty of this. During the first years, we found a mere handful of clients who were willing to try our solution. Once we had some clients as case studies, our sales process became infinitely easier.

COVID-19

During the early days of COVID-19, we had to switch to fully remote customer contact. Fortunately, the energy industry was not as affected as other industries were, and the need to focus on remote sales during the time of crisis has forced us to think outside the box and improve our sales process to be better for rapid scaling - whether or not we're in a pandemic.

hydrogrid.eu

Superdry

TAPKEY

An access platform for property management, car sharing and unattended delivery

FOUNDED	EXPECTED EXIT	INVESTMENT	HQ	SECTOR	EMPLOYEES
2014	MERGER, TRADE/SALE	< 5 MILLION	VIENNA	MOBILE ACCESS CONTROL	11

FOUNDER(S)

Gregor Zehetner (Co-CEO), Markus Minichmayr (Co-CEO), Jochen Schurich (Business Development), Gilbert Hödl (Advisor)

BIO

Tapkey is an open platform for mobile access. It comes with an open application programming interface (API), Mobile and Lock SDK for partners to seamlessly integrate smartphone-based access into existing apps and create new access solutions for a connected world.

FOUNDING STORY

Gregor Zehetner, Markus Minichmayr and Jochen Schurich worked together at Phactum, a software company based in Vienna where Tapkey was born as an innovation project. In 2014, Gilbert Hödl joined the team to complement Tapkey's management team for sales and investment topics. In late 2014, Tapkey was spun out as an independent company. We had to manage office access for changing project teams of up to 40 people. Key handover caused the loss of keys. This led the team to create a prototype that worked via smartphone.

FINANCING

The first four years of Tapkey were bootstrapped by the founders and funded through public grants. In 2017, we raised a seven-digit strategic investment from WITTE Automotive. Today, Tapkey is partially financed by its operative business (software license business, sales of devices and professional services). Additionally, we are in the advantageous position of being able to raise funding in internal rounds if needed, resulting in 80% of shares still being in founders' hands. As the market has been heating up over the last year, we are evaluating further fundraising to accelerate expansion. Tapkey is trusted by a number of internationally renowned partners, such as DOM, WITTE, Skepp, Conrad Connect and Cobot.

MARKET REACH

Tapkey works with different hardware manufacturers with a current focus on the European and Asian markets. In addition, we are in the evaluation process of onboarding new partners to also enter the US market midterm.

WHY AUSTRIA?

Austria is a great location to start a company. It provides a pool of talented software developers, good infrastructure, and high quality of life. Entrepreneurs can seek financial support from public and governmental institutions to master the early phase of starting up. In the past years, Tapkey could repeatedly count on the FFG, AWS, Vienna Business Agency and the Austrian Chamber of Commerce to contribute to Tapkey's path. Access to later-stage investors would help successful startups scale their business globally more quickly.

LEARNING

If we could start over, we would probably focus on B2B integrator business much earlier, as it immediately created a remarkable number of promising leads since we pivoted to this business approach.
One of the biggest challenges we faced was a patent infringement lawsuit filed by one of our European competitors. In 2020, we finally won this dispute and the competitor lost its patent.

COVID-19

Actually, the COVID-19 crisis emphasized the need for contactless access solutions, and that is what our technology stands for; the digital transformation has drastically accelerated and potential new partners have opened up to adopt new technology. Need is the mother of invention: During the lockdown in April, our software engineers developed a hardware simulator for internal purpose to easily test Tapkey-compatible hardware virtually to be more flexible. In the end, this could also be a very useful future product to reduce the development time for our platform partners.

tapkey.com

SUPPORTED BY
go international
Federal Ministry
Republic of Austria
Digital and
Economic Affairs
WKO

txture
txture

TXTURE

A cloud transformation and architecture management platform for enterprises

FOUNDED	EXPECTED EXIT	INVESTMENT	HQ	SECTOR	EMPLOYEES
2017	MERGER, TRADE/SALE, MBO, IPO	1 MILLION+	INNSBRUCK	SOFTWARE, CLOUD, SAAS	16

FOUNDER(S)

Matthias Farwick (CEO),
Thomas Trojer (CTO)

BIO

txture is an end-to-end cloud transformation software platform, guiding organizations on their entire journey to the cloud via readiness assessment, cloud cost estimation and optimizing multicloud environments.

FOUNDING STORY

Matthias and Thomas were closely working together as researchers at the Institute of Computer Science of the University of Innsbruck. The business idea came from scientific research and customer development.

FINANCING

The company has financed itself with early revenue starting from the first month of operation. We also received an FFG Research Studios Austria (RSA) grant as well as venture capital. Our business model revolves around partnerships with large IT consulting companies. The largest partner so far is Accenture, which applies our product globally.

MARKET REACH

We operate globally through partners with clients in Brazil, US, Germany, Switzerland, Austria, UK, France and Japan. Our primary market expansion is growing our business in the US.

WHY AUSTRIA?

At the University of Innsbruck, we were researching the topic of IT transformation and became the starting point for founding our spin-off. The Austrian market has a strong startup community and we have good access to technical talent. Of course, we are always looking for motivated people with enterprise software sales background who want to go global.

LEARNING

Starting over, we would conduct earlier market research and interviews with as many potential customers as possible (i.e. customer development according to Steve Blank). The greatest learning was navigating organizational structures of global companies.

COVID-19

Our product helps organizations reduce costs and risks when moving their IT to the cloud. The topic of cloud transformation was accelerated by the COVID-19 crisis. In fact, we are expecting a net positive effect on our business in the midterm.

txture.io

SUPPORTED BY

go international

Federal Ministry
Republic of Austria
Digital and
Economic Affairs

WKO

HEALTH TECH & LIFE SCIENCES

Even before the 2019-2020 pandemic, Europeans were saying HealthTech is the new FinTech. The Austrian life science, HealthTech and BioTech startups are building on a long tradition of state-of-the-art, ground-breaking research that has been conducted in Austria for centuries. The country's startup ecosystem is currently experiencing a wave of new digital health and HealthTech initiatives as well as being the R&D location for many global players in bioTech and pharmaceuticals. Over 9.2% of startups in Austria consider themselves to be life science companies, according to the Austrian Startup Monitor 2019, and countless university projects have patents and business models waiting in the wings.

“If we could start over, we would be faster in diversifying our product pool.”

ANDMETICS

High-quality, vegan cold wax strips that conform to specific spots on the body make removing unwanted hair easy from the comfort of your home

FOUNDED	EXPECTED EXIT	INVESTMENT	HQ	SECTOR	EMPLOYEES
2014	3-5 YEARS (MERGER, TRADE/SALE)	1.5 MILLION	LEONDING	BEAUTY & PERSONAL CARE	11

FOUNDER(S)
Margot Helm, Andrea Lehner (inventor)

BIO
Through innovative and high-quality products, andmetics empowers men and women with confidence and freedom in the realm of self-care.

FOUNDING STORY
Andrea Lehner (not in the company anymore) and Margot Helm met each other and decided to launch the Brow Wax Strips. Hannes Freudenthaler (Andrea's son-in-law) joined the team as well to cover all relevant skills. Andrea, a make-up artist from Austria, and Hannes invented the Brow Wax Strips.

FINANCING
The company is financed by cash flow and investments. The KMU AG (investment branch of Raiffeisen Banking Group in Upper Austria) has also invested in the company.

MARKET REACH
We are active in more than 20 countries. Our focus markets are Europe, the United Kingdom and the United States.

WHY AUSTRIA?
It is our home country so there was never any question of founding in another country. However, we find wage labor costs to be extremely high and it would be helpful if, for the first years, we would (only) need to pay the employee salaries.

LEARNING
If we could start over, we would be faster in diversifying our product pool and we would try not to depend on one or two large customers for cash flow.

COVID-19
During the COVID-19 crisis, we sold face masks as additional products to existing customers and well-known corporations.

andmetics.com

"We are currently evaluating partnering with large corporations via accelerator programs."

CARBOMED MEDICAL SOLUTIONS

Technology to measure CO_2 levels that transmit data on hormonal changes during female menstrual cycle for women seeking to give birth

FOUNDED	EXPECTED EXIT	INVESTMENT	HQ	SECTOR	EMPLOYEES
2013	4 YEARS (TRADE/SALE)	6.8 MILLION	GRAZ	HEALTHTECH, FEMTECH	12

FOUNDER(S)

Bastian Rüther (CEO), Horst Rüther, Ludwig Wildt

BIO

In 2013 the startup Carbomed started developing a "fertility tracker" for women. The device tests the CO2 contained in the breath - the user breathes into a valve on the device for one minute. More than 3 million euros were invested in developing the device. After crowdfunding and a successful performance at the Puls 4 startup show 2 Minutes 2 Million, production started in mid 2019. In the future, the startup is planning to market the device internationally. Patents for Europe and the USA have already been secured.

FOUNDING STORY

The founding team met during a business meeting before the company existed. The idea came from a collaboration with a university.

FINANCING

The company is financed by grants, loans, leading family offices and venture capital funds. We are currently evaluating partnering with large corporations via accelerator programs (e.g. Merck Accelerator, Startups Meet Pharma, etc.).

MARKET REACH

We are active in three countries. The next target markets are United Kingdom and the United States because of language, market size and purchasing power.

WHY AUSTRIA?

We believe that Austria is a country that provides good grants and well-educated employees. Furthermore, we see a great change for the local healthtech industry by enabling governmental health insurance institutions to invest in promising heahthtech companies. However, we wish incidental wage costs (taxes) were lower for young companies.

LEARNING

If we could start over, we would launch a less complex product at the beginning, bringing it to the market quickly, and continuously extending the features/use cases. The greatest learning has been the importance of finding and keeping the right people for your company.

COVID-19

We were not affected by the COVID-19 crisis.

breatheilo.com

“Austria has a very active medtech community to exchange ideas with.”

CONTEXTFLOW

Deep-learning-based tools improving radiology workflows and empowering radiologists to make effective treatment decisions

FOUNDED	EXPECTED EXIT	INVESTMENT	HQ	SECTOR	EMPLOYEES
2016	N/A	5 MILLION	VIENNA	RADIOLOGY & HEALTHTECH	20

FOUNDER(S)

Markus Holzer (CEO), Georg Langs (Chief Scientist), René Donner (Machine Learning), Allan Hanbury (public funding)

BIO

contextflow empowers radiologists to complete their daily workload faster and with higher quality and cost-efficiency by delivering a unique and scalable AI backbone that fully integrates into clinical workflows. Its core technology includes SEARCH, a 3D image-based search engine, which provides relevant statistics, reference cases and differential diagnosis information at the point of care within seconds. TRIAGE allows radiologists to reorder their worklist based on the presence of specific or time-critical findings. All contextflow's products integrate directly into the radiologist's RIS/PACS.

FOUNDING STORY

contextflow is a spin-off of the Medical University of Vienna (MUW), the Vienna University of Technology (TU) and the European research project KHRESMOI. Founded in 2016, we received the BCS Search Industry Most Promising Startup Award 2016, the 2017 Digital Innovation Award by the Austrian Ministry of Education, Science & Research and were selected as one of 19 startups out of 700+ applications for the 2018 Philips HealthWorks accelerator. Most recently, the Central European Startup Awards awarded us Best Healthcare Startup 2019 - Austria.

contextflow.com

FINANCING

To date, we have received €5 million, mostly from public funding sources. We are supported by four venture capital firms: APEX Ventures, IST Cube, Nina Capital and Crista Galli Ventures. Integrating into hospital workflows is essential for our solution, so we have close partnerships with multiple market-leading medical imaging vendors, to ensure our solution is integrated in a way that it provides value to our joint customers.

MARKET REACH

We are currently working with 14+ partners and customers throughout 7 European countries, before we scale to the US.

WHY AUSTRIA?

Austria has a good startup ecosystem, especially when it comes to supporting innovative high-tech companies with public grants. There's also a very active medtech community to exchange ideas with, and the quality of life in Vienna attracts lots of international talent..

LEARNING

We knew that moving from a research prototype to a certified medical device that actually provides value in the clinical workflow would be difficult, but still we were surprised by its complexity, the time and effort required. We've learned to optimize the roadmap and use a stepwise approach to identifying product market fit and creating a certified medical device.

COVID-19

Prior to the pandemic, we already had the ability to detect COVID-19-related patterns in lung CTs. We quickly developed a version of our 3D search engine (SEARCH) to look for these patterns and quantify the percentage of lung volume affected. Our TRIAGE product also now flags suspected COVID-19 patients. Lastly, we developed an automated pdf report that displays these findings. Thus, we were able to sign two new partner hospitals in Italy in record time. Both were eager to test and validate our COVID-19 features.

SUPPORTED BY
go international
Federal Ministry Republic of Austria Digital and Economic Affairs
WKO

“Our goal is to keep it a family business with strong partners along the value chain.”

DR.OWL NUTRIHEALTH

Dr.Owl NutriHealth develops an advanced technology for the intake of supplements in the so-called health drink category

FOUNDED	EXPECTED EXIT	INVESTMENT	HQ	SECTOR	EMPLOYEES
2014	MBO	2 MILLION	VIENNA	HEALTH SUPPLEMENTS & NUTRITION TECHNOLOGY	5

FOUNDER(S)

Georg Ferdinand Haschke, Ferdinand Haschke

BIO

We are a young, innovative family business with Austrian roots and international orientation in the field of health and nutrition technology (Nutri-Health). We have developed a new generation of health drinks and supplements to boost health and performance through intelligent nutrition.

FOUNDING STORY

Georg Haschke (son) and Ferdinand Haschke (father) founded the company with the aim to make consuming health supplements more efficient and enjoyable. The idea for the first health drink to improve the body's regeneration (Regeneraid®) in times of high strain and stress came during Georg's time in strategy consulting, when he desperately needed this product and started the development of it together with his father, who has a strong background in clinical nutrition.

FINANCING

Initially, the company financing came from strategic investors and since then it has been self-sustaining. We count on our strategic investors from Germany (Döhler Group) for support in developing the tech as well as for their cash investment. We also have a media for equity deal with Pro7Sat1 Group to build the brand in Austria. Our goal is to keep the company a family business with strong partners along the value chain to drive internationalization.

MARKET REACH

Our main market is Austria for proving the business model. We are currently expanding to Germany and Eastern European markets, as well as Central America due to the fitting context for consumer behavior .

WHY AUSTRIA?

Austria was chosen for its stability, workforce, EU market access, and its reputation for quality and innovation. The startup environment could be improved by reducing bureaucracy in governmental support programs for startups and a central support system guiding startups through the vast jungle of options (EU, country, province and city support programs). Austrian companies in general are less willing to make large investments into new technology startups; that is why stronger international ties (within the specific industry - e.g. Pharma) would help.

LEARNING

Our path to a superior delivery technology for supplements was rocky, but great. We believe that maybe we should have made use of government grants and subsidies more often. We have learned to make mistakes, but adopt, adapt and improve faster than our competitors.

COVID-19

The new focus on health topics was a major push for the company: In terms of products, immunity was key. In terms of business model, we focused on our online revenue streams and communication. We adapted each area and it led to record sales.

dr-owl.com

erdbeerwoche

“Our market reach covers the DACH area. Spain and the US are our next target markets.”

ERDBEERWOCHE

The first menstruation-focused social business from Austria, with the aim to make sustainable monthly hygiene mainstream

FOUNDED	EXPECTED EXIT	INVESTMENT	HQ	SECTOR	EMPLOYEES
2011	MERGER, TRADE/SALE	N/A	VIENNA	FEMTECH	5

FOUNDER(S)

Annemarie Harant (CEO),
Bettina Steinbrugger (CEO)

BIO

Erdbeerwoche is the first social business from Austria specialized in menstruation, with the aims of initiating a change in awareness in society and making sustainable monthly hygiene mainstream.

FOUNDING STORY

Bettina and Annemarie founded Erdbeerwoche because they had a vision: The 2 billion menstruating women in the world should not feel ashamed about their period and should have access to sustainable, healthy and affordable feminine hygiene products. Annemarie and Bettina have been working successfully together for more than six years, both in previous jobs in the field of sustainability and now at Erdbeerwoche.

FINANCING

So far, we have financed ourselves by growing organically through sales in our online shop. Some grants and awards (such as Austria's most Sustainable Business Innovation Award, Innovation Space Award, Post Startup Challenge Winner and International Innovation Lab Award) helped us raise awareness about menstruation and sustainable feminine hygiene. We collaborate with several corporations and governmental organizations in the field of female health, digital education and sustainability.

MARKET REACH

Our market reach covers the DACH area (Germany, Austria, Switzerland). Spain and the United States are our next target markets.

WHY AUSTRIA?

Austria has developed a wide startup ecosystem in which every founder can benefit from the support of experts from different backgrounds. We hope for more investment in the ecosystem (e.g. more female investors), a focus in building more international networks for funding, and reducing wage-related costs for young companies.

LEARNING

Advice for every new founder: work with the startup ecosystem, let your vision guide you and always be curious and flexible.

COVID-19

We developed new products and services during the beginning of the COVID-19 crisis, but our international projects will have to be postponed.

erdbeerwoche.com

HELIOZ

Affordable tools for low-income households, humanitarian organizations, emergency aid organizations and companies around the globe

FOUNDED	EXPECTED EXIT	INVESTMENT	HQ	SECTOR	EMPLOYEES
2010	IPO	2.5 MILLION	VIENNA, NEW DELHI	CLEANTECH	9

FOUNDER(S)

Martin Wesian (founder),
Niclas Schmiedmaier (CEO)

BIO

Helioz offers innovative and accessible solutions to improve the everyday lives of those underserved by traditional markets. Its main aim is to provide the target group of over 1 billion people living at the bottom of the pyramid (BoP) with Wadi, a point-of-use device developed to cope with the lack of safe drinking water in many of the world's regions. It uses the power of the sun's ultraviolet (UV) rays to disinfect water in an inexpensive and easy way.

FOUNDING STORY

The idea came from the founders' own experience and the media.

FINANCING

The company is is financed by revenues, founder money, investors' money and grants.

MARKET REACH

The company is mainly active in six countries. The next step is to strengthen the business in target countries like India.

WHY AUSTRIA?

I chose to found Helioz in Austria for governmental research and development funding, the well-educated and skilled workforce, and legal compliance. We hope for more active contact with policymakers, politics and international organizations.

LEARNING

If I could start over, I would reduce the time from research and development to market. I've learned that it is necessary to make good plans and adapt them continuously.

COVID-19

Helioz adapted its services according to the new circumstances.

helioz.org

HOOK
NasdaqListed
HOOKIPA
PHARMA
HOOKIPA Pharma Inc.
HOOKIPA Pharma Inc.
[HOOK]
APRIL 18TH 2019
Offering Price
Offering Size
Nasdaq

HOOKIPA PHARMA INC.

A new class of immunotherapeutics targeting infectious diseases and cancers

FOUNDED	EXPECTED EXIT	INVESTMENT	HQ	SECTOR	EMPLOYEES
2011	IPO IN 2019	~200 MILLION	NEW YORK	BIOTECH	~100

FOUNDER(S)

Rolf Zinkernagel, Andreas Bergthaler, Lukas Flatz, Daniel Pinschewer

BIO

HOOKIPA's proprietary arenavirus-based technologies, non-replicating (VaxWave®) and replicating (TheraT®), induce robust antigen-specific T cells and pathogen-neutralizing antibodies. HOOKIPA's viral vectors target antigen presenting cells in vivo to activate the immune system. Both technologies enable repeat administration to augment and refresh immune responses.

FOUNDING STORY

HOOKIPA was founded in 2011 around the work of Nobel Laureate Rolf Zinkernagel and Professor Daniel Pinschewer with the goal to build a proprietary arenavirus platform for the development of a new class of immunotherapeutics targeting cancer and infectious diseases.
Its co-founder, Rolf Zinkernagel, was awarded a Nobel Prize in Physiology or Medicine for his arenavirus-based work on how CD8+ T cells recognize virus-infected cells. Pinschewer had the foresight to envision a means by which these viruses could be re-engineered to redirect their potent immune response against specific diseases.

FINANCING

HOOKIPA has funded its operations to date primarily from private placements of our redeemable convertible preferred stock, grant funding and loans from an Austrian government agency, and in upfront and milestone payments from Gilead in connection with a research collaboration and license agreement. In June 2018, HOOKIPA entered into a collaboration and license agreement with Gilead Sciences Inc. worth approximately $400 million in milestones and double-digit royalties. The purpose of this collaboration is to develop immunotherapies against HIV and hepatitis B. In 2019, HOOKIPA announced the pricing of its initial public offering (IPO) on NASDAQ, expanding the company's strong shareholder base and raising $84 million in gross proceeds.

MARKET REACH

The company has locations in the USA and Austria.

WHY AUSTRIA?

Vienna as a biotechnology location is an important and competitive center in the European life sciences landscape. The extremely dynamic environment at the international level increases the innovation capacities of the industry. For HOOKIPA, the Vienna location offers an ideal breeding ground for demonstrating the potential and uniqueness of our novel technology and underpinning it with results. Our employees also appreciate the city's excellent quality of life.

LEARNING

The interplay between financing and research is a challenge for life science companies. Usually, the failure rates from idea to product are relatively high. Finding investors at the right time and presenting research results at the right time provide the balance that the management must maintain.

hookipapharma.com

“We believe entrepreneurship should accompany us from the very beginning, ideally starting in kindergarten.”

INSTAHELP

A digital platform for mental health with simplified access to online psychological counseling

FOUNDED	EXPECTED EXIT	INVESTMENT	HQ	SECTOR	EMPLOYEES
2015	MERGER, TRADE/SALE	N/A	GRAZ	EHEALTH	10

FOUNDER(S)

Bernadette Frech (CEO), Martin Pansy (founder)

BIO

Instahelp offers companies or insurance companies an all-around mental health solution: We accompany our customers throughout the entire customer life cycle. From an AI-supported survey of the mental state of health, professional psychological advice online, right through to real-time effectiveness measurement. Instahelp would like to create a supplementary, simple offer to the existing counseling system and it is focused on preventive advice in order to support people before problems even arise.

FOUNDING STORY

The founders started psychological counseling online with Instahelp after developing core competencies in the secure online communication platforms from the exit of a previous startup. We identified a void in psychological treatment online. As we were the first movers in the DACH region with a digital mental health care service, we established strong ties with leading researchers and universities. According to the World Health Organization, every third person is affected by mental health problems. Our vision was to enhance mental health by providing easy access online to professional services.

instahelp.me

FINANCING

The company is financed by angel investors including Toto Wolff, Mercedes Team Principal Formula 1 and Florian Gschwandtner, co-founder of Runtastic. Instahelp cooperates with multiple companies, such as trivago, Lidl, Renault and Klarna, that care about employees' mental well-being. More than 100,000 employees have free access to Instahelp as part of our employee incentive program. Furthermore, we collaborate with insurance companies such as Allianz AT, and LV 1871 Munich/DE, which provide psychological counseling for free for our insurance clients.

MARKET REACH

We are active in five European markets (Germany, Austria, Switzerland, France and the United Kingdom) and aim to foster our on-site presence in Germany and France, as we've received positive market signals.

WHY AUSTRIA?

Austria offers a startup-friendly ecosystem and excellent support to internationalize a purely digital health care service. We believe entrepreneurship should accompany us from the very beginning of our lives, ideally starting in kindergarten. Above all, Austria needs more female founders and female role models in the business world. Research from the Global Entrepreneurship Monitor reveals that Austrians could take more risks and feel more confident in establishing a business.

LEARNING

When we internationalized, we started silently into new markets. Today, we would only enter markets with reliable strategic partners like insurance companies. We care about the psychological well-being of people. Although many people are affected by mental health problems, there is still a strong stigma around this topic. Our biggest challenge is to fight that stigma and to ensure that psychological health receives the same status within our lifestyle as physiological health does. Psychological treatments must become affordable, and prevention should become our focus for a healthy tomorrow.

COVID-19

Instahelp committed to making a strong contribution during coronavirus. Mental health issues are on the rise, and there is a significant increase in psychological counseling on our platform. Furthermore, we made our advanced technology available for medical doctors free of charge to ensure we could provide digital health care during lockdown.

SUPPORTED BY
go international
Federal Ministry Republic of Austria Digital and Economic Affairs
WKO

MYBIOMA

A medtech company that seeks to give everyone access to the most modern microbiome analysis

FOUNDED	EXPECTED EXIT	INVESTMENT	HQ	SECTOR	EMPLOYEES
2018	MERGER, TRADE/SALE, MBO, IPO	1 MILLION	VIENNA	MEDTECH	5

FOUNDER(S)

Barbara Sladek, Nikolaus Gasche

BIO

myBioma makes advanced gut microbiome diagnostics publicly available by providing self-tests based on stool samples. Customers gain access to personalized reports to understand the cause of their problems and improve their well-being.

FOUNDING STORY

Barbara Sladek and Nikolaus Gasche met during a trip to Ghana in 2015. Both were traveling separately there and they stayed in contact ever since. In 2017, they decided to start something new together. Their vision was, and is, to develop new diagnostic tools based on the intestinal microbiome.
Both founders were interested in the micro-universe within everyone's intestinal system for years. They realized that it was difficult for people to receive a validated and well-founded intestinal microbiome analysis. Hence, Barbara and Nic's first idea was to make microbiome analysis available for everyone (including the highest standards, i.e. certified according to ISO 9001 and ISO 13485). With the knowledge gained, myBioma is now developing medical products for specific therapeutic and diagnostic purposes.

FINANCING

We've received funding from public grants, and investors and both founders have invested money, as well.

MARKET REACH

myBioma focuses on the DACH region. However, myBioma is available across Europe and has already shipped analysis to most European countries.

WHY AUSTRIA?

Austria is full of highly trained, talented and smart people in a comparably small area. Having a great team is a crucial success factor for building a company. Moreover, Austria has a multilayered support network for funding and mentoring. This is important to start a company. We also think that, while starting a company in Austria is great, growing a company in Austria is difficult. For larger investments, we have to look outside of Austria. Establishing those connections takes time, which is time taken away from development and new sales and partnerships. Moreover, the legal situation in Austria creates a hurdle for foreign investors to invest large amounts in Austrian startups. A change in conditions there, i.e. more sandboxes, as well as more support from the government in growing a company, would be wonderful.

LEARNING

At the beginning we focused a lot of energy on establishing our own distribution and sales channels. That was a lot of work. Starting over, we would look for alternative distribution channels and focus our energy on something else. Firstly, both founders were surprised to see how much effort it takes to build brand awareness and also maintain a constant level of traction and communication. Moreover, it took some time to understand that a business-to-business approach is more interesting to the European investors' landscape.

COVID-19

myBioma was positively affected by the COVID-19 crisis. Due to the crisis, digital health topics and new medical diagnostic tools became hyped. Moreover, personal health awareness rose. Generally, people are more interested in health-related topics, which is a great benefit and opportunity for myBioma.

mybioma.com

SUPPORTED BY

go international

Federal Ministry
Republic of Austria
Digital and
Economic Affairs

WKO

PLATOMICS

A genetic test that will make personalized medicine as easy and accessible as a simple blood test

FOUNDED	EXPECTED EXIT	INVESTMENT	HQ	SECTOR	EMPLOYEES
2014	5 YEARS (IPO)	3 MILLION	VIENNA	MEDTECH	38

FOUNDER(S)
Albert Kriegner (CEO)

BIO
The company's mission is to make genetic testing available to everyone and to change the way genetic data is managed and analyzed, through game-changing software solutions for personalized medicine.

FOUNDING STORY
The founding team has a long history of private and professional connections, and in a brave and bold moment, the idea to create a startup was born. The founder, Albert Kriegner, was the head of the bioinformatics department at the Austrian Institute of Technology for many years and realized the huge potential for a regulatory compliant digital platform to minimize the enormous workload and costs for laboratories and all stakeholders in the field of diagnostic genetic testing.

FINANCING
The company is financed by grants, founder's money, investors and revenue. We work with Austrian and global providers for genetic testing. They all need a solution that provides both automated workflows for a complex diagnostic device and strategic concepts for the upcoming regulatory requirements.

MARKET REACH
Currently, we are working in several European countries and our product is scalable globally.

WHY AUSTRIA?
Austria has always been at the forefront of medicine. Many innovations were born here. Also, the environment and initial support system for startup companies is attractive. Importantly: Vienna is a city with a high standard of living. That makes it easier for us to get the right people here.

LEARNING
Make no compromises for the hiring of your personnel. Follow every lead. Do not count your working hours. Look at the light at the end of the tunnel.

COVID-19
Since the COVID-19 pandemic, access to partners, customers and stakeholders in general has been difficult, and many investors have halted their activities. However, there is always a way to get to the right people, if you try hard enough. COVID-19 has also affected our team, team culture and team interaction. As a company with a digital focus, it was easier for us to switch to remote work. Still, there is nothing that can replace personal interactions and physical meetings. Until that is possible again, we plan to strengthen our digital communication and use all the available tools.

platomics.com

“As a founder, you want to be as independent as possible, and Austria supports young entrepreneurs quite well.”

REHA BUDDY

to ensure people are staying mobile and independent as long as possible

FOUNDED	EXPECTED EXIT	INVESTMENT	HQ	SECTOR	EMPLOYEES
2019	7 YEARS (TRADE/SALE, MBO)	0.87 MILLION	VIENNA	HEALTHTECH	3

FOUNDER(S)

Harald Jagoš (Co-Founder & CEO), Andrés Tkachenko-Bril (Co-Founder & CTO), Paul Kressnik (Co-Founder & Head of Quality & Regulatory Affairs), Dietmar Rafolt (Co-Founder & Scientific Advisor), Elisabeth Sienčnik (Co-Founder & CFO)

BIO

reha buddy supports patients and medical personnel in the rehabilitation process with a modern tool to ensure treatment transparency and the ability to quantify the patient's individual progress..

FOUNDING STORY

The core members of the founding team previously worked at the Center for Medical Physics and Biomedical Engineering at the Medical University of Vienna . That is also where the idea for reha buddy was born. While researching in the fields of gait analysis and fall detection, we also thought about how to support patients with tele-rehabilitation, especially with smart sensor insoles. As soon as the core-team consisting of Harald, Andrés, Paul and Dietmar committed to develop the initial idea further, we applied to our first incubator (INiTS). That was also when we understood that we lacked critical skills for building business. Since then, our solution has seen major changes while reha buddy's vision is clearer than ever before.

FINANCING

Initially, we received a preseed grant provided by Austria Wirtschaftsservice (AWS), which is now followed by a seed grant since summer 2020. Furthermore, we have just managed to attract our first business angel, who will also become CFO.

MARKET REACH

Currently, we are focused on Austria. We are planning an expansion into neighboring countries, focussing on Germany, Switzerland and Slovenia. In the long run, we see ourselves operating globally, as our solution is scalable and of interest for many stakeholders.

WHY AUSTRIA?

Austria has a rich and active startup community, and you can get lots of help by attending regular meetups and exchanging with other founders. The funding landscape in Austria is very good. There are specific grants for preseed and seed-stage high-tech start-ups, which can provide the essential funding for founders. These grants can be a double-edged sword, since they usually come with above-average bureaucracy and a certain rigidity regarding planning. The IT and innovation readiness of companies and other potential stakeholders is given, supported by a reliable legal framework. Due to Austria's fertile ground for startups, there is a high level of competition.

LEARNING

We would start focusing on building a business much earlier. Developing a solution for a problem and building a product or business are two different things, and it took us some time to realize that.

COVID-19

The COVID-19 crisis affected us directly through shutting down our main target customer (clinics). Therefore, we had to drastically change our sales projections and temporarily focus efforts elsewhere. Before lockdown, we were already making changes to the product and the business model; the COVID-19 crisis gave us the time to look at the business in detail. From today's point of view, it certainly accelerated some necessary changes.

rehabuddy.at

“Setting up new business models in Austria is challenging, as there is a lot of red tape.”

UMMADUM

A points system for ride-sharinge awarding sustainable mobility

FOUNDED	EXPECTED EXIT	INVESTMENT	HQ	SECTOR	EMPLOYEES
2017	IPO	3 MILLION	WATTENS	MOBILITY	10

FOUNDER(S)

Thomas Angerer, Ante Jurcic, Rene Schader

BIO

Ummadum combines carpooling with a points system that rewards driving together. You can be a driver, a passenger or both. With ummadum, you have additional insurance on every trip while not only saving time, but also money. In addition, you reduce traffic, protect the environment and support local retail.

FOUNDING STORY

Rene Schader and Thomas Angerer have known each other since childhood. Years later, they were reunited in Innsbruck and started ummadum. The third founder, Ante Jurcic, has a great international network and was the first supporter of ummadum. Rene Schader is an expert in the mobility and energy sector and was looking into sharing services and their positive impact on the environment, region and personal spending budgets. With those insights, he developed ummadum with Angerer, who relied on his business development expertise network of potential investors.

FINANCING

Ummadum is mainly financed by investors from its parent company, AlphaHapp. We always choose investors with "smart money" - taking into account their network and knowledge in relevant fields. Ummadum was able to attract private investors from the legal, investment and insurance sectors to complement the founders' and employees' skill sets ummadum works with more than 60 active corporations with companies, municipalities and redeem partners that all play a crucial role in the ummadum platform. Companies or public partners purchase a mobility budget (ummadum points) that is distributed among employees or citizens to commute. After using it for sustainable mobility (ride-sharing, bike riding or walking), the mobility budget converts into a shopping budget that can be redeemed at our partners for goods and services. Furthermore, ummadum is participating in several research projects that aim to find and implement innovative mobility solutions for Austria.

MARKET REACH

Ummadum is currently active in Austria and Germany. The parent company, AlphaHapp, will expand into other European countries. The European legal framework and similar customer preferences mean optimal scalability for continent-wide local adoption.

WHY AUSTRIA?

Tyrol was an ideal testing area for the features. Almost all traffic is funneled through the main roads going from west to east, which leads to a lot of shared routes for potential drivers and riders. Additionally, Austria's legal framework allows ummadum to create a template for all of Europe. That being said, setting up new business models in Austria is quite challenging, as there is a lot of red tape that needs to be tackled first - starting from tax law, company law and trade regulations that all require considerable resources.

LEARNING

When ummadum started out, we concentrated on ride-sharing. But over time, we needed to open up to reach more customers. We created features that reward users for biking or walking with ummadum, allowing us to reach a new target group while also adding value for existing users.

COVID-19

Ummadum adapted to the COVID-19 crisis quickly by establishing a new feature - help rides. Help rides enable users to share their route to work, shopping, etc., and nearby users can request help with shopping or other services. This feature also attracted the attention of new partners and was released in cooperation with the food voucher service Sodexo.

FINTECH & REGTECH

The financial technology and regulatory technology sectors are both booming in the EU. Both the Europe-wide introduction of SEPA (Single Euro Payments Area) and the need for streamlined regulatory processes have made Austria and its neighbors hot spots for the FinTech sector and hungry for RegTech solutions to drive efficiency as Europe moves into the future. Just over 6% of Startups consider themselves to be in the FinTech sector, according to the Austrian Startup Monitor 2019.

“Being fast and execution are the secrets of success.”

ABACUS ACCOUNTING TECHNOLOGIES

A turnkey solution for document handling with artificial intelligence for financial and accounting processes

FOUNDED	EXPECTED EXIT	INVESTMENT	HQ	SECTOR	EMPLOYEES
2017	TRADE/SALE	2 MILLION	VIENNA	FINTECH	15

FOUNDER(S)

Christoph Prieler,
Patrick Sagmeister, Ulrich Troeller

BIO

The company is a data science startup serving the accounting industry, providing self-learning software Finmatics for the full automation of accounting data processing to international customers. Its mission is to leverage the AI potential for finance and accounting with easy-to-use AI software.

FOUNDING STORY

The founders knew each other from previous ventures and the idea came to one of the founders through our day-to-day work in large enterprises.

FINANCING

The company is financed though investors, grants and founder money.

MARKET REACH

We are active in seven countries and our next markets include France and the United Kingdom due to their size.

WHY AUSTRIA?

Austria is attractive due to its regulatory stability and the availability of financing for young companies.

LEARNING

We learned that being fast and execution are the secrets of success.

COVID-19

Initially, we were negatively affected, and are now slowly recovering.

abacus.ac

SUPPORTED BY

go international

Federal Ministry
Republic of Austria
Digital and
Economic Affairs

WKO

“The crisis has had a very positive impact on the cryptocurrency market, as people are losing trust in the traditional financial market and fiat currencies.”

BLOCKPIT

Transaction analysis for digital assets with a focus on automated, real-time tax reporting and AML compliance

FOUNDED	EXPECTED EXIT	INVESTMENT	HQ	SECTOR	EMPLOYEES
2017	3 YEARS (MERGER, TRADE/SALE, IPO)	3.2 MILLION	LINZ	REGTECH	17

FOUNDER(S)

Gerd Karlhuber, Mathias Maier, Florian Wimmer

BIO

Blockpit facilitates cryptocurrency tax filing for traders and offers proof of origin when accepting cryptoassets as a bank, exchange or vendor.

FOUNDING STORY

The founders share a similar background of technical studies and working at KPMG. We identified the current problems of digital asset taxation and combined the necessary know-how in regulatory, data analytics and cryptoeconomics to shape the idea of Blockpit. The idea sprouted out of own necessity of the current CEO of the company, who has been actively involved in cryptocurrency trading, mining and other investment activities since 2015. When the BMF issued a clearance paper on cryptocurrency taxation, he found himself facing a high level of complexity when it came to the calculation of his tax liabilities and how to optimize them.

FINANCING

We started by bootstrapping with founders' money and then took the unconventional route with a Security Token Offering (STO), which is the issuance of blockchain-based rights to the company. You can compare this to a "light" IPO, in which we sold 10% revenue participation rights worth €2 million to private investors. These "tokens" can be freely traded on the blockchain and already changed hands a few times since the initial offering. We also held one seed round with a 50:50 equity + token mix, where we onboarded EXF Alpha S.C.S. as our first external shareholder.

MARKET REACH

We are active globally, but strongly focused on the DACH region, US and UK. Next targets are Canada, Australia and South Korea, as they have a high density of crypto traders and strict tax regulation.

WHY AUSTRIA?

As cryptocurrency had a kind of notorious brand around 2017, it was important to base our company in a well regulated and trustworthy country. Also, our existing know-how of the regulatory frameworks in Austria made it easier to get started without worries or uncertainties. The idea of an "Austria Limited" as presented by the government is a great initiative. This makes it easier to introduce work-for-equity models, which can help a lot when starting a company. We believe that in the later stages there should be more incentive for investors to invest their capital within Austria and not in foreign companies or funds.

LEARNING

If we had known how the adoption of cryptocurrency and the upcoming regulation developed in the years from 2017 to 2020, we would have done a lot of things differently - but given there is no crystal ball to tell the future, we think there are few things we would change. The greatest lesson is that everything takes longer than you expect. We had optimistic timelines, which were often disrupted because of external dependences, the market or technical complications. This can result in internal frustration, explanation to investors and financing. Remembering that made planning more reliable.

COVID-19

We have been positively affected by the crisis in two ways: The crisis has had a very positive impact on the cryptocurrency market, as people are losing trust in the traditional financial market and fiat currencies. We were also offered the chance for a COVID-19-related acquisition of our largest European competitor, which resulted in more cooperation and huge growth.

blockpit.io

bluecode

BLUECODE

A European mobile payment solution that combines contactless payment via smartphone with digital value-added services

FOUNDED	EXPECTED EXIT	INVESTMENT	HQ	SECTOR	EMPLOYEES
2017	IPO	35 MILLION	LACHEN	FINTECH	55

FOUDNER(S)
Christian Pirkner

BIO
Bluecode is an easy way to pay by smartphone and at the same time enjoy exclusive benefits without disclosing any user data, all made in Europe. Staff at the checkout simply scan the barcode on your smartphone and you are ready to pay. Vouchers, stamps and loyalty cards are automatically recognized and ensure a seamless checkout experience based on European principles, such as data protection and privacy..

FOUNDING STORY
A successful MVP was already in place. The founding team met through the aws Seed Financing program. The founders noticed that in the payment world a format shift happens, from card to mobile payment, thus the idea was born that this gives Europe a unique chance to become an important player by owning the payment value chain in a world dominated by US payment met hods so far.

FINANCING
The company is financed by the founding team and several European family offices. Bluecode's entire business model is based on partnering with corporations by bringing additional value to their business models.

MARKET REACH
We are active in seven countries, and we focus on growing our core markets (Germany and Austria) to give our users the best payment experience possible. We are also working on European mobile payment interoperability and have co-founded the EMPSA organization (European Mobile Payment Systems Association) to foster collaboration in Europe.

WHY AUSTRIA?
Austria is a central hub in Europe, giving Austrian companies access to top companies throughout Europe. In our case, we have access to some of the biggest banks and retailers in Europe, but we wish for less regulation to let innovation and digitalization happen faster..

LEARNING
Bluecode's partnerships involve retailers, banks and apps with access to a large user base. If we were to start over, we would put more energy into partnering with retailers. The biggest challenge so far has been to overcome the "chicken-and-egg dilemma." It took a lot of creativity, perseverance and energy to solve it andd get to the stage where we are today.

COVID-19
Bluecode is a completely hygienic mobile payment system, so we were able to accelerate our growth during the crisis as our product serves an additional market need right now.

bluecode.com

BSURANCE

Digitizing, individualizing and developing innovative insurance products for checkout systems, applications or online stores

FOUNDED
2017

EXPECTED EXIT
3-5 YEARS (MERGER, TRADE/SALE)

INVESTMENT
4.8 MILLION

HQ
VIENNA

SECTOR
INSURTECH

EMPLOYEES
25

FOUNDER(S)

Franz-Xavier Burner (CSO), Lorenz Gräff (CEO), Manfred Schmiedel (CTO), Andreas Struggl

BIO

With many years of experience in the areas of insurance, sales, project development, marketing and in the digitalization of business, bsurance aspires to lead insurance companies into the future of fully digitized insurance, with self-service platforms and automated processes built for a perfect customer experience.

FOUNDING STORY

The founders knew each other for a very long time and decided to found the company together because of their complementary experiences in the fields of financing, sales, digitalization and technology. We did some research and some interviews, then we tested the idea with a prototype before we founded the company.

FINANCING

The founding team invested €100k and unpaid working hours to bootstrap the company in the first year. Additionally, from the beginning, we could count on corporate venture capital (a convertible and later a Series A). Currently, we are working both on the investment and on the product/sales side, mainly with bigger corporations.

MARKET REACH

We are distributing insurances in the EU + 31 countries (all EU member states and associated countries like Norway and Switzerland).

WHY AUSTRIA?

Two out of three founders were living in Austria and Vienna and it is an attractive place to live, but we think a tax-friendly and easy way to give company ownership to the team would help a lot.

LEARNING

We would start from scratch with an international team, and we would never underestimate the length of the sales cycle in the corporate world.

COVID-19

We believe that in the long term, our business model will win as we deliver a digitalization solution for insurance carriers, but in the short term, we have been hit by sales delays.

bsurance.com

(c) Andreas Müller

"The greatest challenge has been to find the first paying customers and adapt quickly to the needs of the market."

CLEANVEST BY ESG PLUS

A search engine for sustainable investments where private and institutional investors can reconcile their money and their values

FOUNDED	EXPECTED EXIT	INVESTMENT	HQ	SECTOR	EMPLOYEES
2015	10 YEARS (TRADE/SALE)	N/A	VIENNA	SUSTAINABLE FINTECH	11

FOUNDER(S)

Armand Colard (CEO),
Thomas Ebenstein (CTO)

BIO

CLEANVEST is a digital platform that allows private individuals as well as institutional investors to easily identify climate-friendly and socially responsible funds and ETFs in order to invest in them.

FOUNDING STORY

We worked together in the sustainable finance team of the World Wildlife Fund for Nature (WWF) Austria from 2010 onward and spun off into ESG Plus in 2015. We worked on this idea prior to founding ESG Plus or prior to developing the product CLEANVEST.

FINANCING

In 2020, approximately 65% of financing derives from revenues, while the rest is financed via public grants and private investments. Among the paying B2B customers are institutions such as Allianz, Erste Asset Management, BNP Paribas, Liechtensteinische Landesbank, Steyler Bank, Tomorrow Bank, UniCredit Bank Austria, Wikifolio and WWF Austria.

MARKET REACH

We are active in two countries at the moment (mainly Austria with a few activities in Germany). The next target is to expand more widely in the German-speaking DACH region, especially Germany, where in our field of work the market is 26 times larger than in Austria (and Switzerland is 9 times the size of Austria).

WHY AUSTRIA?

Good public funding programs in Austria are a great advantage; however, we think that making founding (e.g. a "GmbH"/LLC) a lot easier than it currently is (or as it was in 2015), specifically by giving shares to employees and substantially lowering the very high non-wage labor costs (*Lohnnebenkosten*) for the first (e.g. 5-10) employees would really improve the ecosystem.

LEARNING

If we could start over, we would begin delegating earlier and giving more ownership to employees (in an earlier stage). The greatest learning has been to ask customers and users for feedback in a very early stage, as we did when we developed CLEANVEST in 2018-2019. The greatest challenge has been to find the first paying customers and adapt quickly to the needs of the market.

COVID-19

In the short-term, we were slightly affected (already some projects have been canceled or postponed), but we expect to be affected more negatively on the mid- to long-term, because the duration of our B2B-sales-cycles is 6 to 18 months (from first contact to closing the deal) and our sales pipeline is not what it normally is (fewer sales opportunities, fewer events and networking opportunities), so we believe that the most challenging times with regard to the COVID-19 crisis lie ahead of us. We have not changed the basic product in response to COVID-19, but we are looking to accelerate the scalability of our product through investing in further automation earlier (e.g. a self-service portal for the B2B segment is planned).

cleanvest.org

SUPPORTED BY
go international
Federal Ministry Republic of Austria Digital and Economic Affairs
WKO

FINNEST

A modern crowdinvesting platform for investment into successful medium-size companies with good, or very good, credit ratings

FOUNDED	EXPECTED EXIT	INVESTMENT	HQ	SECTOR	EMPLOYEES
2014	MERGER	N/A	VIENNA, HELSINKI	FINTECH	25

FOUDNER(S)

Günther Lindenlaub

BIO

Finnest is the leading crowdfunding platform for successful medium-size companies for private investors.

FOUNDING STORY

The idea for the company came from customers' needs and we were quick to execute them. Founded in 2014 by a team of experienced banking and online experts, Finnest plans to offer crowdinvesting for users across Europe.

FINANCING

Very early in 2014, we won an Austrian Promotional Bank (AWS) innovation call, which helped us start. Then, Speedinvest came on board. For the first two years, the founders worked for free. Then, in 2016 we brought some business angels on board. In Q2/2019, the merger with Invesdor Oy happened. We are currently cooperating with advisers and banks who support the company pipeline. We are always open to discussions with partners who find value in providing companies or investors for our platforms.

MARKET REACH

We are active in eight markets, and are strongest in Austria and Germany with our paltform finnest.com and in Finland with invesdor.com.

WHY AUSTRIA?

Each founder is Austrian and with families it was most strategic to remain local.
We think the GmbH is not the best form of corporation if you grow fast (the notary public system does not help either) and we believe that the tax incentive for investments in startups and other alternative investments should be improved.

LEARNING

We have learned to be aware that founding a company is not a sprint, but a marathon. We also learned how important it is to have a great and motivated team around you, and it that is crucial to get the right people on board while the company grows. Everybody counts.

COVID-19

Generally, customers were postponing investment rounds in Q2/2020. We adjusted our offering to reflect the new needs: i.e. building the first digital profit-participation rights *(Genussrecht)* to provide GmbHs with equity and a digital convertible bond to minimize the negative effect on lower company valuation. On the investors' side we fortunately did not recognize a decrease in interest.

finnest.com

“The idea was to simplify the way business verification is done and make it accessible to everyone through technology.”

KOMPANY

The industry leader in providing real-time audit-proof business verification data for all business KYC (KYB) needs

FOUNDED	EXPECTED EXIT	INVESTMENT	HQ	SECTOR	EMPLOYEES
2012	TRADE/SALE, IPO	14 MILLION	VIENNA	REGTECH	50

FOUNDER(S)
Peter Bainbridge-Clayton, Russell E. Perry

BIO
Kompany is a RegTech platform for global business verification and business know your customer KYC (KYB). We operate a proprietary global live network that provides real-time access to official commercial and banking registers, covering over 110 million company records in more than 200 jurisdictions.

FOUNDING STORY
The founders first met in 1998 while working at mobile operator ONE in Vienna. As we spent time successfully building next generation networks and mobile services, it was a natural next step to create something brand new once again. We worked in more than 40 countries and always struggled to verify our business partners, suppliers or merger and acquisition counterparts in an efficient and effective way. The idea was to simplify the way business verification is done and make it accessible to everyone through technology.

FINANCING
The company's financing can be described in the following timeline: Founders seeded the startup, business angels then funded the product development stage and now institutional investors are supporting the growth stage. kompany is an alumni of the Mastercard Start Path Program, the Oracle Startup Program and the Raiffeisenbank International FinTech Partnership Elevator Labs Program Elevator Labs. We have also partnered with corporations through F10, Plug and Play Tech Center, FinTech Frankfurt and Abu Dhabi. Raiffeisen Bank International has become our first major enterprise customer and is now also a shareholder and investor.

MARKET REACH
We have customers in more than 115 countries. Our core markets are Europe, USA and the Southeast Asian economic centers. kompany is headquartered in Vienna with sales teams in London, New York and Singapore. A full rollout in North America is our next target.

WHY AUSTRIA?
Compared to other international locations, there are no benefits in founding a tech company in Austria. We would like legislation to be adapted in several areas. For example, allowing greater employee particiaption by the granting of employee stock options without creating a taxable event and moving tax liabilities to the time of exit. We need quicker red-white-red work permit processing, as the three-month average does not allow us to compete with international tech hubs. Finally, we should have tax incentives for investments from Austrian trusts and introduce an Anglo-Saxon style company structure (e.g. limited company, or mini-AG).

LEARNING
If we could start over, we would have founded the company in the US and established a branch office in Austria. Our main challenge was to anticipate the timing of when the addressable market would adapt to new AML regulation. In Europe, the main business driver was the EU's 4th AML directive that went into effect in 2017. Only in 2018 did we see the market demand full compliance services to fulfill these compliance requirements, which otherwise would risk billions of euros in fines.

COVID-19
We did not adapt our product or business model. We were positively affected by the COVID-19 crisis as the government economic stimulus programs increased the need for business KYC (KYB) and anti-money-laundering checks. Additionally, before the COVID-19 pandemic, the European Union's 5th anti-money-laundering directive went into effect in January 2020, which increased the regulatory requirements simultaneously.

kompany.at

"We learned to have transparent decision making and good internal communication in order to have all team members on board."

MOBILE-POCKET

The mobile loyalty & rewards platform is a marketplace for retailers, brands, wallet providers, payment services and app users

FOUNDED	EXPECTED EXIT	INVESTMENT	HQ	SECTOR	EMPLOYEES
2001	MBO	DISCLOSED SERIES	HAGENBERG IM MÜHLKREIS	FINTECH	53

FOUNDER(S)

Roland Sprengseis, Wolfgang Stockner

BIO

mobile-pocket has proven itself as a global loyalty app and loyalty platform. With its popular B2C app users always have their loyalty cards and offers at hand. The Platform has been created to address the B2B sector. It allows to manage loyalty cards, sign up processes for loyalty programs, mobile payment and to deliver offers through tailored targeting options directly to the connected clients.

FOUNDING STORY

The founders were university peers. Long-term customers asked us to develop a single customer solution. We matched the dots and developed a licensable product instead of a single customer project. That affected pricing and benefits on both ends. We took the risk, which turned out to be the right decision.

FINANCING

The company runs on its revenues. We have a wide set of corporate customers. Furthermore, we co-developed a product suite called "rewards" with Vodafone Group that sets a global standard in reducing churn rates for mobile network operators. We have also partnered with a double-digit number of banks to digitalize value-add services in the field of mobile payments.

MARKET REACH

mobile-pocket is available worldwide and the app is translated in 13 languages. We currently have six strong markets. We are in a strong wave of expansion into a new region.

WHY AUSTRIA?

There is a strong customer base in all segments concentrated in a small geographical area, and skilled developers are available "around the corner." As Austria is among the countries with the highest quality of living worldwide, it is a great place to found your company and attract international staff to hire. Located in Central Europe, Austria is also well connected to all relevant hubs in Europe for developing your business. There is also strong financial support from government and public institutions, if the goal is international expansion.
However, we would improve tax incentives for investors, lower cost of work for the first three years or a certain company size and focus on education and creating an ecosystem for specific industries, which suit the competitive advantages as a country (e.g. tourism and tech, biotech, education and tech, farming and tech, etc.).

LEARNING

We think we would have selected specific projects with a stronger focus on the core goal; we would also have changed our fundraising routine and gained more international shareholders in target markets. We learned to have transparent decision making and good internal communication in order to have all team members on board; focus on core tasks only and share projects and opportunities with your competitors when these do not fit your focus, because your "competitors" usually are not your competitors, but rather your partners in establishing a new market segment.

COVID-19

During the lockdown, we digitalized the final sales processes, all other processes were already set up in a way that allows remote working. We also sped up the development of a new solution suite for SME's, as demand in this segment increased exponentially.

hub.mobile-pocket.com

SUPPORTED BY

go international

Federal Ministry Republic of Austria Digital and Economic Affairs

WKO

"It's a digital financial fitness coach that helps people build better financial habits, financial buffers and save money for concrete targets."

MONKEE

We make saving money fun with your own personal finance coach, helping you achieve your goals and stay motivated

FOUNDED	EXPECTED EXIT	INVESTMENT	HQ	SECTOR	EMPLOYEES
2019	N/A	0.8 MILLION	INNSBRUCK	FINTECH	8

FOUNDER(S)

Jean-Yves Bitterlich (CTO), Martin Granig (CEO), Christian Schneider (COO)

BIO

Monkee is a Tyrolean startup that shows what saving can look like in the age of digitization. The founders' vision is to help people improve their financial health and make them financially fit by making saving as easy as spending money.

FOUNDING STORY

We knew each other for more than 15 years, as we both have been in senior management positions within the same premium consumer goods organization. Both share a passion for technology, stock trading and have a strong entrepreneurial spirit. Our experience ranges from fitness trackers to digital products that use gamification to help people feel better. We realized that financial fitness is a big issue, as physical, mental and financial health are highly connected. Money worries are the No. one factor for stress and are negatively impacting physical and mental health, relationships and work performance. Therefore, we decided to use our experience to develop a digital financial fitness coach that helps people build better financial habits, more financial buffers and save money for concrete targets.

FINANCING

The company is financed by founder money, angel investors and government grants.

MARKET REACH

Monkee is currently available in kick-off markets Austria and Germany. The current setup allows us to offer services across the whole EU, but international expansion is planned only after the next fundraising round in order to have proper financing for marketing activities.

WHY AUSTRIA?

Austria was chosen for the availability of a range of government grants to kick-start the project and lever initial investments by founders, and for the rather small, but high quality, startup ecosystem that helps to create a certain visibility within the Austrian scene. We wish for more incentives that would encourage investors to invest in Austrian startups, better access to highly talented software developers and a more entrepreneurial-friendly society. Today, entrepreneurs are seen as greedy and exploitative in Austrian society, a completely different situation in contexts like the USA.

LEARNING

If we could start over, we would increase our focus even more at the really essential elements of the MVP. We say we could develop an even simpler MVP to go to market even a bit earlier and develop everything else based on feedback and data from real users. We also would have sought startup mentors earlier, as founders have a lot of experience in the corporate world.

Our biggest challenge was that we knew we could not realize our concept without the right banking partner. We were a small team with a great idea, yet banks did not take us seriously, and it was very difficult to get a bank on board that could handle our requirements to realize our concept. We discussed several times that we could not progress with the app development and we would need to stop the project in case we could not find a partner. We leveraged all personal contacts until we found the right partner and could continue with the development.

COVID-19

As Monkee is currently fundraising, we realized that finding investors might be more difficult after COVID-19. Therefore, we further streamlined our cost structure, slowed down build-up of resources, postponed some developments and increased focus on development of key features that might be more relevant after COVID-19 (e.g. FutureBoost). Positive changes due to COVID-19 are that customer growth accelerated, as the use case of financial health is more relevant than ever – people are more aware that financial buffers are important (e.g. short time, lost jobs, etc.).

monkee.rocks

SUPPORTED BY

go international

Federal Ministry
Republic of Austria
Digital and
Economic Affairs

WKO

“We wanted to make blockchain technology accessible to the general public.”

TMIA

TMIA and its product, NodeVenture, stores cryptocurrencies safely and profitably.

FOUNDED	EXPECTED EXIT	INVESTMENT	HQ	SECTOR	EMPLOYEES
2019	IPO	0.4 MILLION	LINZ	FINTECH	11

FOUNDER(S)

David Schnetzer, Cagdas Tasdemir

BIO

Through the secure storage of digital assets, we make blockchain technology accessible to the general public.

FOUNDING STORY

David previously worked in the financial sector and Cagdas came from the IT industry. They were aquainted for a long time due to social circles and joint work on a database project. Later, both started to play a key role in the biggest Ethereum mining farm in Central Europe. This was the beginning of their belief in Blockchain technology. The two wanted to make the use of the innovative blockchain accessible to the general public. The first use case of blockchain technology was Bitcoin. A hype about the crypto currency broke out, which also attracted more and more cyber criminals and fraudsters. Trying to build a bridge between the present and the future, the prospective company starters found that the biggest challenge was to make the storage of digital assets simple, scalable and impossible for hackers to penetrate. With the development of the patented „Multi-Layer-Security" technology, combined with an „Air Gapping System", David and Cagdas finally set the bridge piers in stone.

FINANCING

TMIA GmbH is financed by a combination of AWS, FFG, KGG UBG, business angels and a research award. We want more than sponsorship; we want a long-term partnership. Our partner has to be confident to take the step forward with blockchain technology and to have confidence in us.

MARKET REACH

At the moment, we are focused on the Austrian market. The next target markets are Switzerland and Germany because we already have a promising network and once you have established yourself in the DACH region (Germany, Austria and Switzerland), you will be able to expand into other, less well-known markets with a broader base.

WHY AUSTRIA?

Austria is located in the middle of Europe, which is why the location offers a promising geographical starting point for further expansion. In addition, there is legal stability and access to Eastern Europe, an interesting market with great potential. There are helpful funding opportunities for young companies. For founders, priority treatment in visits to the authorities, search for investors, registrations, checks, etc., would be an improved condition, because in the early stages, time can be a key factor that decides survival.

LEARNING

If we could start again, we would probably start fundraising earlier and more intensively, also internationally. For this purpose, we should have contacted accelerators more quickly. First of all, you need a good business plan, which you should keep to. In the early stages a good network is also essential. Especially in our industry, you have to deal with a lot of legal and compliance issues, which cost time and money. Another time waster is bureaucracy and dealing with authorities. You have to realize that certain processes simply take time.

COVID-19

Since we are in FinTech, working from home was not an issue, because this possibility existed before the crisis; we were hit by the fact that our potential partners became more reserved for fear of a longer crisis or similar reasons. The willingness to invest decreased, which delayed our go-to-market plans.

tmia.at

SUPPORTED BY

go international

Federal Ministry Republic of Austria Digital and Economic Affairs

WKO

WIKIFOLIO

Invest just like a trader – without having to do anything yourself

FOUNDED	EXPECTED EXIT	INVESTMENT	HQ	SECTOR	EMPLOYEES
2012	TRADE/SALE, MBO, IPO	12 MILLION	VIENNA	FINTECH	40

FOUNDER(S)
Andreas Kern

BIO
On wikifolio.com, private and professional traders present their personal trading strategies. Each trading strategy is made completely transparent in a virtual portfolio – the wikifolio.

FOUNDING STORY
I came up with the idea while receiving a consultation at a bank, when they tried to sell me a "compelling" product.

FINANCING
The company is financed through angels, venture capitalists and partners. We have created an ecosystem around wikifolio.com with banks, issuers, exchanges, asset managers and media companies. Visibility is generated through our user-generated content or wikifolios created by companies themselves.

MARKET REACH
We are active in Germany, Austria and Switzerland and wikifolio certificates are listed on the Börse Stuttgart Exchange as well as on the BX Swiss.

WHY AUSTRIA?
Vienna is one of the most beautiful cities in the world, but lower or no taxation of stock options would represent a great improvement.

LEARNING
We learned to focus more on human resources, including recruiting and culture. We were very successful early on, however, we did not evaluate our progress closely enough before investing in new features or markets.

COVID-19
The company has been positively affected by the situation, with more new users and more trades.

wikifolio.com

HRTECH & EDTECH

When it comes to human resources and education, Austria has a number of tech solutions that facilitate recruiting and help students get the most out of their schooling and studies. Globally, (also in light of the pandemic) the EdTech market is predicted to see annual growth of 18% per year over the next decade, according to a July 2020 study by Grand View Research. Recruiting is also becoming a hot topic as a PwC survey shows that 74% of companies plan to increase spending on HR Tech in 2020 to address pressing talent needs.

FIRSTBIRD

A digital employee referral program optimized to leverage your company's and employees' networks

FOUNDED	EXPECTED EXIT	INVESTMENT	HQ	SECTOR	EMPLOYEES
2013	2 YEARS (TRADE/SALE)	4 MILLION	VIENNA	HRTECH	50

FOUNDER(S)
Arnim Wahls (CEO), Daniel Winter (CTO), Matthias Wolf (COO)

BIO
Firstbird connects firms offering jobs and companies worldwide with suitable candidates. With Firstbird, employees become brand ambassadors, and referrals become a company's most successful recruiting channel.

FOUNDING STORY
The founders knew one another through personal and professional connections. We were working in recruiting before founding Firstbird and experienced firsthand how broken the process is.

FINANCING
The company is financed by investors. Corporates are our target customers and we were lucky to partner with big players, including SAP, Oracle and Deloitte.

MARKET REACH
We offer our software as a service (SaaS) in 15 languages, which is used from the United States to China. We have a strong focus on large European markets and opened our APAC operations in Sydney in 2020.

WHY AUSTRIA?
Vienna is a great city to live in and is attractive for international talent. However, access to capital in Austria should be improved alongside decreases in bureaucratic and financial burdens when operating a GmbH.

LEARNING
If we could start over, we would put the pedal to the metal much faster, generating more funding and senior hires from day one. We believe that growing from 10 to 50 people changes your culture, your processes and especially your role as founders.

COVID-19
We launched an additional product to support customers who were facing large rounds of layoffs during the COVID-19 crisis.

firstbird.com

SUPPORTED BY

go international

Federal Ministry Republic of Austria Digital and Economic Affairs

WKO AUSSENWIRTSCHAFT AUSTRIA

THE
ONE THA
STARTE
IT ALL

FRETELLO

Use technology to learn how to play guitar and seamlessly adapt to your progress along the way

FOUNDED	EXPECTED EXIT	INVESTMENT	HQ	SECTOR	EMPLOYEES
2016	3-5 YEARS (MERGER, TRADE/SALE)	1.125 MILLION	LINZ	EDUTECH	25

FOUNDER(S)

Wolfgang Damm, Florian Lettner

BIO

Fretello uses artificial intelligence to listen to your playing and seamlessly adapt to your progress, giving you the feedback you need to become the best guitar player you can be.

FOUNDING STORY

The founders knew one another from university. One of the two is a self-taught guitar player who always struggled to progress. I did not have access to a good teacher and despite trying really hard to get better, I was practicing the wrong things the wrong way. Sure, there are tons of YouTube lessons out there. None of them could really teach you something, though. Moreover, all the online courses have one thing in common: Videos do not give you any feedback. Being a software engineers and having a strong background in digital signal processing, we decided that it had to be possible to find a solution that helped identify the right exercises, analyze performance, and provide tailor-made practice plans and workouts according to personal progress.

FINANCING

Thanks to our work for 360-degree camera manufacturer VSN Mobil, we were able to bootstrap Fretello. We re-invested our revenue and, in combination with grants from the Austrian Research Promotion Agency, we we created our audio technology and entered the market. An early investment from startup300 helped us reach product-market fit and validate our business model shortly thereafter. Fretello licenses music copyrights from publishers and labels globally. We have deals with Sony/ATV and Kobalt/AWAL, who own a majority of global music copyrights.

MARKET REACH

We are active globally. Our main markets are the United States, Central and Western Europe, followed by Russia and Japan, which, alongside eastern countries, are emerging fast. There is huge demand for mobile learning resources and learning a musical instrument is part of social identity.

WHY AUSTRIA?

We asked ourselves: "What are the benefits of founding a company in the United States? Do we have to be in Silicon Valley? And for what purpose? Is there anything we can do there which we cannot do in Austria?" The honest answer was no. Sure, it is much easier to get venture capital elsewhere, but also development costs are much higher. However, Austria would benefit from changing bureaucracy, taxes, grants, investor relations and venture capital funds. We think we have a good network of business angels and early-stage grants, but when it comes to scaling, there are few chances in Austria. The willingness to take risk on both sides (investors and founders) is still quite conservative, even if your KPIs are good. There are too many conditions connected to grants: You have to reach milestones and you get a small installment. What startups mostly need is growth capital in the beginning so they can experiment, learn, fail fast, learn again and grow.

LEARNING

We would try to do things faster. Set up hypotheses and validate them, move on with what works, not waste too much time on things that do not work as we initially thought. Building a remote-first company and hiring talented people regardless of nationality, culture and time zone are most challenging, but also some of the most rewarding things we could have hoped for.

COVID-19

We did not adapt our product because of the COVID-19 crisis. The EduTec sector was one of the winners of the crisis; people had more time to learn something new while staying at home.

fretello.com

“The lack of access to quality teachers is one of the most fundamental problems in education globally.”

GOSTUDENT

A dynamic online learning platform with virtual classrooms, clear organization and afterschool tutoring

FOUNDED
2016

EXPECTED EXIT
4 YEARS (IPO)

INVESTMENT
8.5 MILLION

HQ
VIENNA

SECTOR
EDTECH

EMPLOYEES
100+

FOUNDER(S)

Gregor Müller, Felix Ohswald

BIO:

GoStudent builds the no 1 global school by connecting students with the best teachers via individual tutoring sessions. Thus, GoStudent is the perfect partner for both parents and kids by encouraging sustainable successes along the entire education path.

FOUNDING STORY

The founders first met at the age of 15 because they shared a circle of friends. Later, both founders studied in Switzerland and, after returning to Vienna, shared ideas about different problems they wanted to tackle. I was lucky my grandfather was a great teacher. Through his tremendous skill to share not only the passion for different school subjects but also always finding a real life application, showing me how to use theory, he had a huge impact on my future career. The lack of access to quality teachers is one of the most fundamental problems in education globally. We wanted to change this by connecting children to world-class teachers in a virtual learning environment.

FINANCING

Our investors are Leftlane Capital (New York), DN Capital (London) and Speedinvest (Vienna). In total we raised €15 million.

MARKET REACH

We are active in Germany, Switzerland and Austria. In October, we opened our first international office in Lyon. We are currently preparing a market launch in Spain. More European countries will follow in the coming years.

WHY AUSTRIA?

We chose Austria for the high quality of life, the more affordable talent compared to Berlin or London, and good flight connections within Europe.

LEARNING

At the very beginning, we had a great idea and no monetizable business model. We would put more focus on building our business model. We have learned that the product alone is worth nothing - you need to find ways to really get to your target audience (either by great sales or great marketing or both).

COVID-19

We pivoted at the end of 2018 when we shifted the focus of our marketing and sales efforts toward parents of children ages 6-19. The COVID-19 crisis was an accelerator for the whole digital education industry, including us.

gostudent.org

SUPPORTED BY
go international
Federal Ministry Republic of Austria Digital and Economic Affairs
WKO

“Putting good people into good jobs.”

HOKIFY

Putting quality people into quality jobs in the fastest and most enjoyable way possible

FOUNDED	EXPECTED EXIT	INVESTMENT	HQ	SECTOR	EMPLOYEES
2015	N/A	3.5 MILLION	VIENNA	HR TECH	47

FOUNDER(S)

Karl Edlbauer, Daniel Laiminger, Simon Tretter

BIO

hokify is an Austrian startup specializing in the recruitment of professionals in the tourism, catering, craft and commercial sectors.

FOUNDING STORY

We met while studying business and economics at the Vienna University of Economics and Business. We started our venture in the course of a class at the SIMC Master Program. We experienced difficulty when searching and applying for jobs through mobile devices. Furthermore, we realized how painful the search and application process was in general, as companies relied on endless numbers of online forms with dated and non-intuitive user experience.

FINANCING

The company is financed by business angels, strategic investors and grants. Our strategic investor is the leading job portal in Austria, Karriere.at.

MARKET REACH

We are active in Germany, Austria and Switzerland.

WHY AUSTRIA?

We chose Austria for its access to high-quality talent and accommodating landscape for early stage funding, grants and subsidies. In order to generate large and globally active startups, the Austrian startup ecosystem would require more later-stage funding opportunities. In order to make large series A, B, and C funding rounds, most startups have to rely exclusively on foreign investors.

LEARNING

Starting over, we would focus even more on user feedback, especially at the beginning, in order to prevent too many product pivots to find a product market fit. Furthermore, we would risk the expansion even earlier in order to grow even faster. Team and culture are key in order to build a successful startup. The product and the market might change, but the team and the culture of the team are key for adapting to change and becoming a successful startup in the long run.

COVID-19

The crisis has decreased the volume of published jobs in general during the lockdown and increased the insecurity over how the economy develops. However, shortly after the first restrictions were lifted, the market started to grow again and we benefited from the pay-for-performance factor in our business model, since recruiting budgets were invested with more caution.

hokify.com

SUPPORTED BY

go international

Federal Ministry Republic of Austria Digital and Economic Affairs

WKO

"Monetizing is essential for every startup, but sacrificing early revenues for a better-working product is the right thing to do."

MIMO

A fun and interactive way to learn how to code, build apps and much more, regardless of the experience and time you have

FOUNDED	EXPECTED EXIT	INVESTMENT	HQ	SECTOR	EMPLOYEES
2016	N/A	N/A	VIENNA	EDTECH	25

FOUNDER(S)

Henry Ameseder (COO), Johannes Berger (CEO), Dannis Daume (CTO), Lorenz Schimik (CPO)

BIO

At Mimo, we're teaching the world how to code, and we're building the best way to learn while doing so.

FOUNDING STORY

Struggling to learn coding as a teenager and later seeing many undergraduates at the Technical University of Vienna made me realize there had to be a better way to learn to code. At the time the founder started with an idea that eventually became Mimo, I was looking for help in certain areas, namely, design, content and development. I met my co-founders through friends, Product Hunt, as well as job postings. We had never met before and worked together loosely for a year before deciding to go all in and build a company together.

FINANCING

The company is financed by revenue, investors and grants.

MARKET REACH

We are active worldwide via the App Store and Google Play Store.

WHY AUSTRIA?

All co-founders are Austrians and lived in Vienna. We see much talent in the area of development and product in Austria or a willingness to relocate to Austria. For other positions, it is quite tough to hire in Austria. For an improved startup ecosystem in Austria, we would expect a better structure for companies compared to the expensive and heavy GmbH, and an easier way to attract talent to Austria instead of the lengthy Red-White-Red card process.

LEARNING

By now, we understood that we need to focus on the users first and build the right product for them instead of scaling revenues from day one. In the beginning, we did not pay enough attention to how well the product worked for users after they subscribed. Monetizing is essential for every startup, but sacrificing early revenues for a better-working product is the right thing to do if the financial situation allows for it. Otherwise, it could be dangerous to become too dependent on revenues and not care about the user experience as much.

COVID-19

We were positively impacted by the fact that the whole education sector moved a step closer to being digital. We had a digital product from day one and did not need to adapt.

getmimo.com

ROBO WUNDERKIND

Learn to code through the joy of play

FOUNDED	EXPECTED EXIT	INVESTMENT	HQ	SECTOR	EMPLOYEES
2014	MERGER	N/A	VIENNA	EDTECH	16

FOUNDER(S)
Rustem Akishbekov, Anna Iraotska, Yuri Levin

BIO
Robo Wunderkind builds tools that change the way kids play, learn, and create with tech in school and at home. Our award-winning robotics kits empower kids aged 5 and up to learn to code through the joy of play.

FOUNDING STORY
Our founders met in 2013 at an event called "Pioneers Festival" in Vienna, where tech geeks and entrepreneurial spirits meet to join forces and network. Robo Wunderkind was conceived as an idea to help empower children to explore their creativity through learning to code, understanding the basics of robotics, and seeing that the world around them is waiting to be explored and constructed with the help of technology. We believe that sensible tech education can prepare children to be the model citizens of the world of tomorrow. They will be confident, inventive, tech-savvy, STEM-proficient, empowered to create things and having the self-assuredness to do so.

FINANCING
The company is financed through grants, bootstrapping, business angels and venture capital. We cooperate with many distribution partners worldwide, many of which are multinational corporations.

MARKET REACH
We are active in more than 20 countries through our partners' network. Our next target market is the United Kingdom because of the considerable spending on the education sector and a high level of adoption of educational technology tools.

WHY AUSTRIA?
Founding a company in Austria opens great access to a pool of very talented people with an innovative and international mindset. The governmental support, especially during early founding stages, is profound. In Austria, founders can get early-stage seed financing through a variety of grants, which makes bringing ideas to life much easier. Finally, an excellent quality of life is another great advantage. However, we believe that easier access to funds for late-stage financing rounds would make a great difference for us and would help them scale faster.

LEARNING
Looking back, we would put more emphasis on customer development in the beginning when the idea of Robo Wunderkind emerged. During our development, we witnessed a need for more in-depth research on our target customer segments and their motivations - we had to catch up on this knowledge before our idea became a physical product in customers' hands. Now, we are continuously working on understanding our customers with rigorous research and testing. One of our greatest challenges was scaling the team and processes once we had resources and capabilities to do so. We had to grow from a small team with very ambitious ideas, to involving senior, growth-oriented leaders, which was the single most important thing that helped us achieve success.

COVID-19
In response to the dramatic need for homeschooling activities caused by school closures, our products were enhanced with a variety of online as well as physical content. We launched the Robo Makers Marathon, a 10-week series of online workshops around coding and robotics, in which parents and children could join for free. Educators also benefited from special teacher webinars, expanding their professional development and learning how to integrate coding and robotics in their classrooms. The COVID-19 crisis posed a challenge of selling our products to schools, but opened new doors for business-to-consumer market - parents and children.

robowunderkind.com

SUPPORTED BY

go international

Federal Ministry Republic of Austria Digital and Economic Affairs

WKO

TEAMECHO

A working environment that allows everyone in a company or organization to unfold their full potential

FOUNDED	EXPECTED EXIT	INVESTMENT	HQ	SECTOR	EMPLOYEES
2015	MERGER, TRADE/SALE	0,31 MILLION	LINZ	HR-TECH	20

FOUNDER(S)

Markus Koblmüller, David Schellander

BIO:

TeamEcho is the real-time mood barometer for organizations to keep track of employee satisfaction and company culture with an agile feedback tool.

FOUNDING STORY

I was organizing startup meetups in Linz and David Schellander joined one disucssion. We became friends, and when we were confronted professionally with the problem of lack of communication between managers and their employees, we asked Schellander if he would like to be the designer in the team to work on a solution for this problem. The design part soon shifted to become part of the management. We recognized that communication between employees and their managers is suboptimal. On the one hand, personal conversations rarely provide honest feedback; on the other hand, traditional employee surveys are very time-consuming, offer only one-time insights and are hardly relevant to act upon. The result is employees quitting their jobs, increased sick days and demotivation, which leads to massive costs and loss of revenue. We wanted to find a sustainable solution to tackle this problem.

FINANCING

For the development of the first prototype, we won Catalysts (now Cloudflight) - one of the largest companies in the field of custom software development in Austria - as a partner, who provided development services in the form of work-for-equity. Together with Catalysts and supported by public funding, we bootstrapped TeamEcho until the beginning of 2019, mainly financed by revenues. After that, we raised our first business angel investment in April 2019. We work closely with Catalysts/Cloudflight, from whom we continue to source development services. We also have partnerships with companies in the field of organizational development that use TeamEcho with their customers.

MARKET REACH

We are currently targeting the German-speaking area. Nevertheless, TeamEcho is used in foreign subsidiaries of our customers from Vietnam and Nigeria to the United States. In addition to Germany, Austria and Switzerland, we will soon be starting activities in selected European countries.

WHY AUSTRIA?

As a business location, Austria distinguishes itself by its outstanding public funding for innovative companies. It may be more difficult to find private investors, but it is easier to attract public funding. Since there are great innovations in Austria (but they rarely reach the size of those in the USA), we believe it is necessary to facilitate access to external growth financing. To ensure this, politicians should work on making investments in Austrian startups more attractive.

LEARNING

If we were to start all over again, we would think bigger from the beginning, raise investment earlier and start scaling. Looking back, we think we lost too much time in the first few years. What we often find difficult is making decisions with uncertainties. To decide for or against something under difficult conditions is an issue we are still working on. Considering how great the risk of making the wrong decision is, it is a challenge that we have not yet fully mastered.

COVID-19

In order to use the crisis as an opportunity, we released a free version of TeamEcho in the first week of the lockdown to measure sentiment on the crisis and home office. This enabled us to generate a lot of leads in the short term, although there was hardly any new software investment on the customer side at the beginning. Overall, we believe that the crisis will help us, as TeamEcho brings great added value, especially for dipersed teams, which are now on the rise.

teamecho.at

SUPPORTED BY

go international

Federal Ministry Republic of Austria Digital and Economic Affairs

WKO

“Building a company means building relationships. Despite how it may seem, you cannot do it alone.”

WISR

Enterprise software manage retired employees with an aging workforce

FOUNDED	EXPECTED EXIT	INVESTMENT	HQ	SECTOR	EMPLOYEES
2017	MERGER, TRADE/SALE	0.8 MILLION	VIENNA	HR TECH	6

FOUNDER(S)

Klaudia Bachinger (CEO),
Martin Melcher (CTO), Carina Roth (CFO)

BIO

WisR started off as a job platform for retirees and recently added a B2B software supporting enterprises to stay in touch with their retired employees in order to secure company and industry knowledge and strengthen their brand.

FOUNDING STORY

During her professional career in journalism, Klaudia produced a documentary on future trends in which she gained research knowledge on the future of work, silver society and the gig economy. After experiencing elderly depression in her own environment and spending her 30th birthday with retirees, she decided to build a platform connecting retirees with companies for project-based and part-time work. So she actively started looking for two co-founders to complement her skills and met Martin at a Smart Ninjas coding school and Carina Roth at an incubator for chatbots and AI (Lemmings.io).

FINANCING

We received a public grant first and then got business angels on board. We also have a commission-based sales cooperation with the consulting firm Mercer in Austria, introducing us to relevant clients.

MARKET REACH

We started off with our job platform for retirees in Austria and Germany, but our enterprise software solution is international since our clients are often global players.

WHY AUSTRIA?

WisR chose Austria due to the availability of public grants, lower rents and salaries compared to Germany, the UK or the US. The high quality of life in Vienna attracts talent from abroad, especially tech talent from the CEE region.
However, to improve the climate for startups in Austria, our team wishes for a GmbH-light, with more risk capital, one address/format only for public grants, tax cuts on employee salaries, and shares (ESOP), and last but not least, a faster way to get working permits for non-EU talents, as we believe the Red-White-Red Card is a good idea, but poorly executed.

LEARNING

If we could start over, we would opt for a GmbH-light and better evaluate all alternatives when it comes to founding. As far as entrepreneurship goes, we would probably try to be even leaner and experiment with no-code solutions before starting development. As far as investment goes, we would try to only raise money with convertibles as long as possible - a quicker, cheaper and smarter way. We have learned that it is crucial to have a great co-founding team and a good relationship with investors. Building a company means building relationships. Despite how it may seem, you cannot do it alone, and everything takes twice as long and costs twice as much.

COVID-19

WisR had to adapt. Since it was a period with low recruitment volumes, we focused on our enterprise solution instead. It allows companies to offboard their employees into retirement respectfully and stay in touch with them for knowledge transfer and temporary job engagements.

growwisr.com

"We are aware that there is no perfect solution to completely avoid the trial-and-error phase."

WORKHELD

Intuitive workforce management for maintenance, customer service and manufacturing

FOUNDED
2015

EXPECTED EXIT
MERGER, TRADE/SALE, MBO, IPO

INVESTMENT
N/A

HQ
VIENNA

SECTOR
SAAS SOFTWARE

EMPLOYEES
10

FOUNDER(S)
Benjamin Schwärzler

BIO
WorkHeld is a software platform that increases the efficiency and transparency of industrial processes with innovative technologies and user-friendly apps.

FOUNDING STORY
The founder Benjamin came up with the idea while working as a CAD (computer-aided design) engineer during an internship and while looking for a COO with industry expertise. By luck he met Christine as she was leaving ThyssenKrupp and moving to Vienna.

FINANCING
The company is financed by investors, Austrian Research Promotion Agency (FFG) grant and revenue. Kapsch BusinessCom invested in 2019 and is now a sales partner.

MARKET REACH
Most of our business is in Austria and Germany, but we are now starting to sell outside of the DACH region (Germany, Austria, Switzerland), with our first project in Slovenia.

WHY AUSTRIA?
We praise Austria for its stable environment and its motivating startup scene. We think that access to a mocked "enterprise data set" would help founders be more successful.

LEARNING
If we could start over, we would sharpen the product vision earlier in order to move faster later on. We are aware that there is no perfect solution to completely avoid the trial-and-error phase. We have learned to master business-to-business enterprise software sales.

COVID-19
We started to change their business model from direct sales to partner sales before COVID-19 and the crisis accelerated this change.

workheld.com

STARTUP.ROADMAP

We are by your side from the idea through to scaling your company.

WORKSHOPS, MENTORING & COWORKING

FROM MARKET ENTRY TO GROWTH

Once a year | 3 months | Wattens
growthcamp.at

FROM BUSINESS MODEL TO MARKET ENTRY

Twice a year | max. 18 months | Innsbruck
startup.tirol/booster

FROM IDEA TO BUSINESS MODEL

Twice a year | 6 months | Innsbruck
inncubator.at/innc-programm

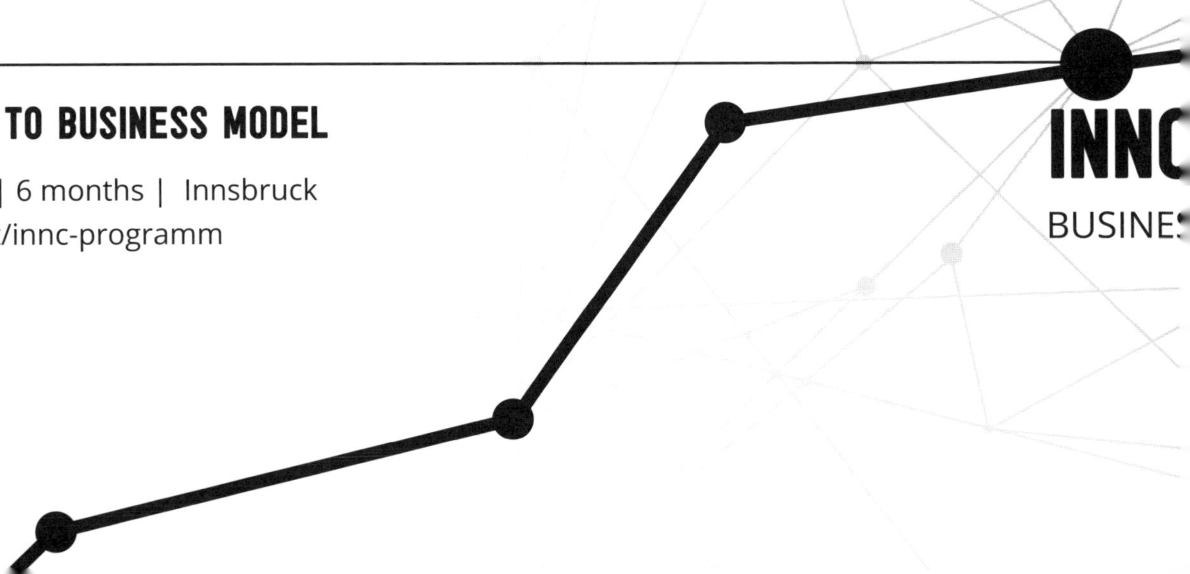

MARKET-PLACE & ECOMMERCE

From sports platforms and streaming tools for social media to refurbished devices and fulfillment services, this category has experienced a big boost due to pandemic safety measures. While this category does not include ecommerce for existing shops or brands, many offer B2B solutions to help businesses deliver goods and services to remote customers. More than 11% of startups in Austria identify as offering ecommerce and marketplace services, according to the Austrian Startup Monitor 2019.

“Austria is a great location to start a marketplace for outdoor activities!”

CHECKYETI

An online platform that allows you to search for, compare and book winter and summer activities across Europe

FOUNDED	EXPECTED EXIT	INVESTMENT	HQ	SECTOR	EMPLOYEES
2015	TRADE/SALE	10+ MILLION	VIENNA	ONLINE TRAVEL	50

FOUNDER(S)
Stefan Pinggera, Georg Reich

BIO
CheckYeti is the largest online platform to book activities in 1,000+ mountain and beach destinations across Europe - including skiing, rafting, mountain biking, paragliding, boat trips and more. CheckYeti enables holidaymakers and outdoor enthusiasts to experience seasonal activities with their ideal guide.

FOUNDING STORY
The two founders went to school together and have been friends since then. After university and several years in banking/consulting, we spoke about creating a business of our own. In our experience, organizing a ski instructor is time-consuming and inconvenient. We decided to create an online booking platform for winter sports activities, which very quickly grew to a pan-European marketplace for outdoor activities.

FINANCING
We started CheckYeti with founder money, after which we financed the company's growth with the support of business angels and venture capital. We have ongoing marketing partnerships with several corporations in the outdoor and travel industry, primarily online travel agencies, but also traditional tour operators.

MARKET REACH
We are currently generating revenue in 20 countries with a focus on European summer and winter holiday destinations. Attractive new markets include holiday hot spots in Asia-Pacific, the US and Latin America.

WHY AUSTRIA?
Austria is in the heart of the Alps, which makes it a great location to start a marketplace for outdoor activities. Besides the vibrant startup and angel investor community, we experienced that Vienna is a good place to hire talented and motivat-ed native-speakers from Italy, France and Spain, which playedan important role in our international expansion.
One thing that would help for sure is to keep pushing an entrepreneurial mindset early on in the education system and continue to promote startup culture and successes in higher education across disciplines (medicine, technology, business, etc.). This would widen the pool of people who are motivated and qualified to start their own businesses or work in key positions in early-stage companies.

LEARNING
We started with a well-intended vision, but it was too small in the beginning. We only realized over the years the full potential of our product and our market. If we would do it again, we would "think big" right from day one. One transition has been particularly interesting: growing from a smaller team, where every member can be directly managed by one of the founders, to a team size where this is simply not feasible any longer. Many of the elements that make a startup succeed cannot be pushed forward by the founders alone anymore. Instead, much of our focus as a founder moves toward hiring and coaching other people to take over that role and responsibility in managing their own teams.

COVID-19
Same as other travel companies, the COVID-19 crisis brought our business to a halt at the end of Q1 2020. Considering the circumstances, we believe that we were lucky, though, as the "outdoor tours and activities" segment was among the first ones to recover well during the summer of 2020.

checkyeti.com

“We quickly adapted our software to offer online streaming and on-demand videos to present our partners and prospects with a way to make money during the crisis.”

EVERSPORTS

Eversports enables people to do their favorite sports, wherever they are, whenever they want, everytime and everywhere

FOUNDED	EXPECTED EXIT	INVESTMENT	HQ	SECTOR	EMPLOYEES
2013	3 YEARS (IPO)	12 MILLION	VIENNA	SAAS-ENABLED MARKETPLACE	65

FOUNDER(S)

Philipp Braunsberger, Hanno Lippitsch, Emanuel Steininger

BIO

Eversports is a marketplace where sport providers and athletes are easily connected. The innovative Web Portal and Mobile App make it simple to filter and set priorities for sports you are eager to play. Our goal is to provide the community with social functions to help with planning of sport sessions.

FOUNDING STORY

We got the idea when one founder was trying to book a tennis court online and ended up having to call five locations before he found one that had availability at the time he was looking to play. We quickly realized that this problem not only is applicable to tennis, but also for sports in general.

FINANCING

We raised €12 million in angel, seed, Series-A and our last bridge round. Additionally, we are in two double equity programs and are adding government-backed loans to the mix. We acquired Uniqa Ventures as an investor, helping us through difficult times. We are still trying to find ways to cooperate with Uniqa and other corporates, but it requires a great deal of time investment and ideally a dedicated team to make it work, which we could not yet put in place.

MARKET REACH

We are currently operating in seven markets in central and western Europe. In 2021 we hope to further expand our market leadership position in German-speaking markets, and become market leader in Netherlands, Belgium and France. Our next target markets have not been decided yet, but the UK and US are very interesting options.

WHY AUSTRIA?

Public funding and incubators helped us during our first couple of years. Having a startup in Vienna is not like having one in Berlin, when it comes to the "war for talent." We are not saying it is easy to find tech-talent in Vienna, but from what we heard from friends and colleagues in more hyped startup cities, it is easier and more affordable here. However, improvements in Austria could include more programs in schools and universities showing what entrepreneurship is about. In the first years, we realized how much worse a "nonemployed" person is treated by banks, insurance etc. vs. "regular employees". Despite the founder having valuable shares in the company and a regular decent income, few banks would provide a loan to buy an apartment.

LEARNING

If we were to start over, we would have made plenty of changes, especially with the knowledge of creating popular software. We should have said "no" more often, instead focusing on the things that show traction, especially after having a product-market fit, but this is still difficult today as there are so many opportunities that look exciting at first. The greatest lesson was how important it is to always be and stay close to customers.

COVID-19

In the first weeks, COVID-19 hit our company hard since most of our partners' sport centers and studios closed during lockdown. Sales told us that demos were canceled and no one was interested in software, but people were still looking for ways to stay in shape. When we quickly adapted our software to offer online streaming and on-demand videos, we could present our partners and prospects with a way to make money during the crisis. We quickly averted initial losses and could get our whole team out of short-time work after three months.

eversports.at

SUPPORTED BY

go international

Federal Ministry Republic of Austria Digital and Economic Affairs

WKO

INFLUENCE.VISION

Facilitating the collaboration of advertisers and content creators

FOUNDED	EXPECTED EXIT	INVESTMENT	HQ	SECTOR	EMPLOYEES
2017	MERGER, TRADE/SALE	N/A	VIENNA	INFLUENCER MARKETING	18

FOUNDER(S)

Florian Bösenkopf, Branko Markovic

BIO

influence.vision is an influencer media ad network taking influencer marketing to a higher level with a visionary marketing platform.

FOUNDING STORY

Starting as startup scouts in the United States after finishing our studies in finance, we founded the Vienna AdNetwork and presented a more innovative way of influencer marketing.We quickly realized we wanted to move into the tech industry, leading to our first platform project, which we then sold in order to move to Silicon Valley working for Bosch. In the US, we both experienced the rapidly moving social media industry firsthand. At a Silicon Valley Café, Bill's, the idea and the logo were born (on a napkin).

FINANCING

influence.vision is financed by a strategic investor. The partnership between influence. vision and the exclusive advertising time marketer of Mediengruppe RTL is intended to demonstrate how TV advertising and influencer marketing can pull together and how advertisers can be offered even greater coverage.

MARKET REACH

Today, influence.vision is active in five countries: Austria, Germany, Switzerland, Italy, Slovenia and Croatia.

WHY AUSTRIA?

Sitting in the heart of Europe has some major advantages for influence.vision. The most important one is availability of qualified specialists. As a tech company, customer-centricity is at the top of our mind. Highly qualified specialists are crucial to ensure an excellent customer experience. To improve the startup environment in Austria, it would be most important to adapt the legal structure. Founding a company is complex enough. Areas like taxation, accounting, formation of a company, incentives (e.g. virtual stock options program) should be changed and simplified to become advantageous for founders.

LEARNING

Culture is key. Especially in startups like influence.vision. Putting more emphasis on corporate culture and underlying guidelines is crucial for a company's success. Building an organizational structure was our greatest challenge, with many hidden challenges you would never think of before you do it on your own.

COVID-19

influence.vision was negatively affected by COVID-19. Due to the crisis, we have pivoted our strategy away from pure growth and toward holistic customer centricity. Customer success is at the top of their priority to ensure sustainable company success.

influencevision.com

SUPPORTED BY

go international

Federal Ministry Republic of Austria Digital and Economic Affairs

WKO

"We offer every streamer the opportunity to get the best out of themselves and their stream."

OWN3D

An international media agency and internet platform for esports and game streaming

FOUNDED	EXPECTED EXIT	INVESTMENT	HQ	SECTOR	EMPLOYEES
2018	N/A	475,000	STEYR	HR LIVE STREAMING	19

FOUNDER(S)
Andy Hanne, Lukas Hoffmann, Thomas Rafelsberger

BIO
OWN3D was founded in 2017 to make the world of live streaming more colorful. We offer every streamer the opportunity, including tools, services and products, to get the best out of themselves and their stream. Our product caters to expert streamers and newer users, working with all streaming platforms, such as Twitch, YouTube, Mixer or Facebook, and all streaming software, such as OBS Studio, Streamlabs, StreamElements or BEBO.

FOUNDING STORY
We met in a Facebook group for online marketing. The idea spun out of the founders' personal experiences as streamers.

FINANCING
It is financed by investors, and we are currently cashflow-positive.

MARKET REACH
We have sold our digital products to more than 130 countries with an export rate of 98%. In 2021 will release our products in China, South Korea and Japan.

LEARNING
We learned early on to focus on our strengths and to get people on board who are strong in what you are weak in.

COVID-19
Online media in general was positively affected by the COVID-19 crisis from an economical perspective.

own3d.tv

SUPPORTED BY
go international
Federal Ministry Republic of Austria Digital and Economic Affairs
WKO

PIXELRUNNER

The world's first outdoor print robot turns a landscape into an advertising medium at a quality, speed and cost efficiency never seen before

FOUNDED	EXPECTED EXIT	INVESTMENT	HQ	SECTOR	EMPLOYEES
2016	5-8 YEARS (TRADE/SALE)	1.3 MILLION	HAGENBERG IM MÜHLKREIS	MARKETING, ADVERTISEMENT	4

FOUNDER(S)

Rainer Kargel, Ronald Schaumberger, Christian Saminger

BIO

The company provides qualitative landscape printing for sports and large-scale events, landscape and flight lane advertising, guidance systems and floor lettering. Pixelrunner handles large area landscape printing as a full-service provider. We transfer the motif into a large area printable format, advise customers on the perfect implementation and print the motif onto the desired substrate on site. In the medium term, we also intend to sell the equipment worldwide via a rental model.

FOUNDING STORY

The idea of Pixelrunner, an autonomous robot for large format printing, was born in 2013 when Schaumberger and Saminger identified a business opportunity in the field of sports events. Previously, logos, messages and images were rudimentarily "brushed" onto the surface using stencils. By means of "rough prototyping," a first test setup was created. A converted weed sprayer on a tractor was the result, with the aim of turning the landscape into a woven support using an automatic printing process. Finally, in 2016, Pixelrunner GmbH was founded as an advertising company.

FINANCING

The company is financed by a mix of equity contributions from its seven shareholders, non-repayable grants or loans, especially from R&D activities and order processing.Pixelrunner works with leading brands such as Red Bull, ABB, BMW, Julius Bär, Lagerdère and Pirelli, but also major events like the Berlin Marathon and Vienna City Marathon.

MARKET REACH

Currently, Pixelrunner generates revenue in eight countries: Austria, Belgium, Germany, England, Italy, France, Switzerland and Spain. In 2021, we plan to expand our services to more European countries. In 2022, the company plans to expand to North America.

WHY AUSTRIA?

It is important to us that the Pixelrunner generates 100% added value in Austria. We make sure that we only use Austrian materials as much as possible, i.e. material, human resources, construction, engineering and assembly. To improve the startup ecosystem, our team would like changes in the regulatory environment, including less bureaucracy and fewer costs for GesmbH and GmbH.

LEARNING

If we could start over, we would focus more on the core product, without being overly detail-oriented. The biggest challenge has been the range of requirements and tasks for a small team (technology, color development, market launch, etc.). However, we are sure that if we go step by step, it will work out in the end.

COVID-19

Since we generate most of our revenue from the event and sport industries, COVID-19 is affecting us severly.

pixelrunner.com

SUPPORTED BY

go international

Federal Ministry Republic of Austria Digital and Economic Affairs

WKO

“Our goal is ... to contribute to a more sustainable world and offer a better alternative to new and used products on the market.”

REFURBED

The fastest growing marketplace for renewed products in German-speaking countries, with up to 40% cheaper and 100% more sustainable products

FOUNDED	EXPECTED EXIT	INVESTMENT	HQ	SECTOR	EMPLOYEES
2017	5 YEARS (MERGER, TRADE/SALE, IPO)	18 MILLION	VIENNA	MARKETPLACE	>100

FOUNDER(S)

Kilian Kaminski, Jürgen Riedl, Peter Windischhofer

BIO

refurbed is a platform for highly reliable refurbished products, with high and uniform standards in terms of quality, safety and guarantee. In this way, consumers can buy used devices without taking risks themselves. Our goal is to make refurbished products popular throughout Europe, to contribute to a more sustainable world and offer a better alternative to new and used products on the market.

FOUNDING STORY

The founders met in the Austrian startup scene and two of them already knew each other from the university. Each of the founders was working in a similar field. Kilian was leading the refurbished-products program at Amazon in Germany. What connected the founders was that they wanted to create a company that changed the world in a positive way.

FINANCING

We did three rounds of funding with international investors. So far, we have had limited success with partnerships, as big corporates are too slow and not flexible enough.

MARKET REACH

We operate in Germany, Austria, Italy and Poland, and will be launching in several more countries in Europe in the coming months.

WHY AUSTRIA?

Austria has a small startup scene, which is great at the start, since many people want to help and you quickly build a reputation. Austria also presents our biggest challenge in the long run, as there is limited available talent compared to Berlin or London.
For an ideal startup environment, we wish for less bureaucracy - no notary appointments, simpler legal forms, no fees for publishing company changes in Wiener Zeitung - and lower salary taxes. We would stop most grants and reduce the taxes for salaries paid to founders and employees of startups.

LEARNING

We might invest more in product and less in marketing and we understood that everything is always a people business, so you need to have the best people and enable them to do their best work in order to be successful.

COVID-19

We were positively affected by Covid-19, with more people buying electronics online.

refurbed.at

SUPPORTED BY

go international

Federal Ministry Republic of Austria Digital and Economic Affairs

WKO

“We are bringing a largely analog industry into the digital age and offering customers technical solutions to buy and sell scrap metal.”

SCHROTT24

Digitizing the metal recycling industry in Germany and Austria to help companies reach environmental and sustainability goals

FOUNDED	EXPECTED EXIT	INVESTMENT	HQ	SECTOR	EMPLOYEES
2016	3 YEARS (MERGER, TRADE/SALE)	4+ MILLION	GRAZ	SCRAP TRADE	18

FOUNDER(S)

Alexander Schlick, Jan Pannenbäcker

BIO

Schrott24 is the largest digital trading platform for scrap metal.

FOUNDING STORY

The circular economy has never been a more important issue for the planet. This is only exacerbated with the ever-growing global demand for raw materials. The metal recycling industry plays a central role in achieving our environmental and sustainability goals; not only can it be almost fully recycled, there is no limit to how many times. However, the current status quo is simply inefficient and unacceptable. Positive changes can only come about through innovations in this old-fashioned industry. That is why we made it our business to completely turn the entire industry inside out. We are bringing a largely analog industry into the digital age and offering customers modern processes and technical solutions to buy and sell scrap metal in a more efficient way.

FINANCING

Our first round of financing was done with startup300 in 2017. Since then, we have had a couple of international investors join, such as Gisbert Rühl, CEO of Europe's largest metal merchant Klöckner; FJ Labs, a renown business-to-business marketplace investor from the US; and Fil Rouge Capital. We also received grants from regional, national and international institutions. The largest amount was a €1.2m innovation grant from the European Commission, the EIC accelerator.

MARKET REACH

Schrott24 operates a platform for the purchase of scrap metals in Germany and Austria. However, we are selling the material Europe-wide and in some cases overseas. We help scrap dealers, recyclers and factories in our European network to increase their capacity utilization and gain new suppliers. We now have over 400 logistics and recycling partners across Europe, as well as over 80 delivery points for scrap metal in Germany and Austria.

WHY AUSTRIA?

The biggest benefit of founding in Austria is the access to grants, especially in the early founding stages. Especially since COVID-19, the regionality becomes less relevant, as conferences and meetings move online. In Austria, the competition for talent is smaller, as is the talent pool. For us, the biggest issue in Austria is the mindset. We believe we need to embrace a culture in which no one is stigmatized if she or he fails and also praise and support each other, be happy about the success of others, and not only our own. To get there, it would be helpful to teach very practical entrepreneurship courses.

LEARNING

It is always easy to say with hindsight, but it is important to iterate faster, be more data- and test-driven, and build an A-class team as soon as possible. We cannot pinpoint one specific lesson, but we believe it is important to be humble and explore solutions by going on a journey and iterating.

COVID-19

Like many other industries, the scrap metal trade was hit hard by the consequences of the corona pandemic in 2020. Production levels dropped dramatically, as did liquidity in the industry. While the situation was and remains challenging for us, there are some new opportunities. The market is looking more at digitalization and as the prime actor in our industry, we receive additional attention. We were also able to ship our first software as a service (SaaS) product, a white-label sourcing web shop for scrap dealers.

schrott24.at

“We built a complete, self-hosted online shop within 48 hours in order to address new target groups with additional products, which met great success!”

DIE STOFF-SCHWESTER

An ecommerce solution for wide varieties of fabrics

FOUNDED
2014

EXPECTED EXIT
IPO

INVESTMENT
N/A

HQ
VIENNA

SECTOR
eCOMMERCE AND BRICK & MORTAR (RETAIL & WHOLESALE)

EMPLOYEES
7

FOUNDER(S)

Candice Barlow, Ernst Buchmann

BIO

Die Stoffschwester is an online shop where you can purchase fabrics for adults and kids.

FOUNDING STORY

It all started with a pregnancy and a sewing machine, and the desire to express our own creativity in the form of in-house production. The founding team created a company and took a close look at what was already available and how it was implemented. Our main focus was to transform a stationary shopping experience into ecommerce retail.

stoffschwester.at

FINANCING

The company was fully funded by the founders; its growth made possible by cash flow, and profits were reinvested. This meant slower growth, but the advantage was that the company kicked off the very first minute. The concept immediately yielded income and we have grown into a reliable commercial business. We worked closely with another company to launch an information and sales fair, exceeding expectations with over 6,000 visitors over three days.

MARKET REACH

We currently have only one branch in Austria. However, due to ecommerce, the location is not decisive. We sell our products worldwide, primarily targeting the EU. Germany is our second most important market after Austria. Our next target market will be France. If we open a second branch, it would most likely be in Germany or Holland.

WHY AUSTRIA?

Due to family responsibilities, there were no alternative locations. For companies that are strongly moving toward digitalization, Austria can be disadvantageous. In Austria, founders face many obstacles, starting with trade regulations that are not up to date. The employee protection regulations no longer fit into today's times. GDPR also represents a competitive disadvantage for European companies. The Austrian Chart of Accounts is disadvantageous because the inexpensive software from Germany cannot be used. The Cash Register Ordinance, which was not available in English for a long time, forces Austrian retailers to resort to solutions that are more expensive. Austrian banks have their own solution for account access. Also, the Austrian startup community needs to be publicly presented in a more positive way.

LEARNING

We believe we should have pushed expansion faster, and an earlier focus on the use of an enterprise resource planning tool would have made things easier.

COVID-19

We were positively affected by the COVID-19 crisis. Our products were increasingly sought after. We built a complete, self-hosted online shop within 48 hours in order to address new target groups with additional products, which met great success!

SUPPORTED BY
go international
Federal Ministry Republic of Austria Digital and Economic Affairs
WKO

“Do not make promises that cannot be kept, give facts and keep the timelines you make for yourself.”

VENUZLE

An online marketplace and enterprise management solution for municipalities, local councils, clubs and schools.

FOUNDED	EXPECTED EXIT	INVESTMENT	HQ	SECTOR	EMPLOYEES
2014	TRADE/SALE	0.6 MILLION	GRAZ	SAAS	6

FOUNDER(S)
Wolfgang Lang

BIO
The vision of Venuzle is to make planning and coordinating sports activities user-friendly and suitable for everyone, to increase everyone's motivation to stay active. At the same time, sports providers are given the opportunity to optimize their management, communication and distribution channels, as well as simplifying manual processes and increasing the utilization.

FOUNDING STORY
The founding team got together as friends who saw a gap in the market as active football players trying to organize spaces to play.

FINANCING
The company is bootstrapped and financed by investors.

MARKET REACH
We are active in the DACH region (Germany, Austria, Switzerland). We might expand to English-speaking countries in 2022.

WHY AUSTRIA?
We chose Austria for its access to public funding. However, we wish it was easier to access venture capital and larger sources of funding.

LEARNING
Starting over, we would spend more time creating contracts with co-founders. We learned that more clients means more work - so do not make promises that cannot be kept, give facts and keep timelines you make for yourself.

COVID-19
We adapted our product only marginally as the COVID-19 crisis affected us both negatively and positively.

venuzle.at

WE SHIP FULFILLMENT

Fulfillment means helping dealers, entrepreneurs and doers to better reach their customers with good shipping solutions

FOUNDED	EXPECTED EXIT	INVESTMENT	HQ	SECTOR	EMPLOYEES
2018	7-10 YEARS (TRADE/SALE)	1 MILLION	GRAZ	eCOMMERCE FULFILLMENT	15

FOUNDER(S)
Manuel Wagner

BIO
The perfect storage and logistics solution for companies of all sizes.

FOUNDING STORY
The founding team got to know each other while working together at other companies or on previous projects..

FINANCING
The company is financed by investors.

MARKET REACH
Our current market includes Austria and Germany, which are where we keep warehouse locations.

WHY AUSTRIA?
Our primary wish for a future startup climate in Austria is easier access to growth capital.

LEARNING
We learned to be faster and never underestimate the demands and importance of administrative tasks

COVID-19
Covid-19 has had both positive and negative effects.

weship.at

VERBUND X ACCELERATOR

FRANZ ZÖCHBAUER
Director Corporate Innovation and New Business, VERBUND AG

Franz Zöchbauer, VERBUND's head of corporate innovation spoke to the 100 Startups team about how startups in the energy, mobility and infrastructure sectors can benefit from their network, customer base and ecosystem.

What sectors and innovation areas is VERBUND looking for?

In our innovation strategy, we have defined clear focus areas in which we aim to achieve new growth: Green Hydrogen, New Storage, Digital Energy and Electric Mobility Furthermore, we are committed to supporting innovation activities in our core business of generating electricity from hydropower as well as wind and solar energy.

In June 2020, we launched our new VERBUND X Accelerator as a new energy and infrastructure innovation platform. Together with leading Austrian companies and international partners, we want to work with the best startups around the world in order to implement innovations faster. It was important for us to take into account the new situation resulting from the Corona crisis. For this reason, we and our partners have also included the topic "Infrastructure of the Future" as a central topic area in VERBUND X Accelerator. This was also the area that attracted the most interest from startups.

How is the accelerator program organized, what can startups expect?

In designing the VERBUND X Accelerator program, VERBUND has specifically focused on cooperation with industry and ecosystem partners. We can solve the energy and infrastructure challenges of the 21st century better and faster together, which is why our alliance offers exciting cross-sector market opportunities for the participating startups. But it also opens up new perspectives for the participating companies as they innovate.

Startups can expect VERBUND and its strategic partners to finance concrete pilot projects and deliver a joint proof-of-concept. If the projects are executed successfully, there will be many further opportunities for cooperation and market development.

Are there any further startup engagements planned?

Yes, definitely. Our startup engagement programs are an important component in the implementation of our innovation strategy. In 2020, w had over 1,100 applications fro startups around the world. We worked together with 40 startups in innovation bootcamps.

It is important for us to obtai concrete results from these collaborations in order to creat something new together. To th end, we will continue to work intensively and focused with startups in the future.

Please reach out if you are interested in shaping the futur of energy together.
linkedin.com/in/franzzoechbaue

Find out more!

INNOVATIO

/ɪnəˈveɪʃ(ə)n/ nou

1. the action or process of innovati

"innovation is crucial to the continuing success of any organizati

2. VERBUND's Innovation Symphony mo

All tools and measures reflect a strong sense of collaboration ins and out, strengthening the company in its entirety. VERBUN innovation ecosystem approach is also reflected in the way th cooperate with external partners. Be it the innovation partnership w the Stanford NPL affiliate program and Austrian universities startup accelerator programs with strategic partne

MOBILITY & ENERGY

From scooters, bikes and electric vehicles to tracking software, mobility and energy have been hot topics in Austria for years. Both Vienna and Graz have large-scale smart city projects and the market for renewable energy solutions and optimization is strong and growing. In Austria, renewables account or over 1/3 of energy consumption, with hydro and wind leading the ways for the smaller solar and biomass sources. According to the Austrian Startup Monitor 2019, 5.3% of startups in Austria classify themselves as working in these sectors.

“With the help of our global community, we strive to be the perfect navigation for bikes, becoming the #1 app for cyclists worldwide.”

BIKEMAP

Providing community-generated cycling maps and navigation services on a global scale

FOUNDED	EXPECTED EXIT	INVESTMENT	HQ	SECTOR	EMPLOYEES
2014	7 YEARS (IPO)	3 MILLION	VIENNA	MAPS & NAVIGATION	20

FOUNDER(S)

Peter Eich, Helge Fahrnberger, Christof Hinterplattner

BIO

Founded in 2014, Bikemap was created by passionate cyclists with the goal of sharing awesome routes with cyclists around the world. Until today, more than 3.8 million users have created over 6.1 million unique cycling routes in 100+ countries worldwide.

FOUNDING STORY

Speedinvest invested in our seed round. Since then, we have experienced multiple rounds with both new and incumbent investors. The idea came from Peter Eich, a touring cyclist. The current CEO is not the founder, as the new CEO took over 2.5 years ago.

FINANCING

Currently, we can count on a mixture of grants and investors. With our online shop, bikemap.net, it is possible to buy custom-made smartphone mounts for bikes, made in Austria by our partner BikeCitizens.

MARKET REACH

We are active in essentially all countries with available app stores. We are growing interest in new focus markets, including the US and the Southern Hemisphere.

WHY AUSTRIA?

Austria was a smart choice in which to found because of its quality of life, infrastructure and grants. We wish there was less institutional fragmentation, as we consider Austria too small to have such a complicated system.

LEARNING

One lesson we acknowledged over time is the importance of being 100% focused on what we have in front of us.

COVID-19

We doubled down on building the best cycling app in the app store. After an initial, negative effect in March and April 2020, we have been positively affected by the situation.

bikemap.net

“BikerSOS focuses on scaling, but we take the phrase ‘If you fail, fail fast’ to heart”

BIKERSOS

An accident detection and emergency alarm for motorcyclists

FOUNDED	EXPECTED EXIT	INVESTMENT	HQ	SECTOR	EMPLOYEES
2016	N/A	N/A	LINZ	SAFETY	4

FOUNDER(S)

Bernhard Aichinger, Christian Indra, Werner Richtsfeld

BIO

BikerSOS detects falls automatically and sends an emergency call. With the products of BikerSOS you are prepared for your next ride and get the fastest possible help in an emergency.

FOUNDING STORY

The founding team knew one other for several years prior to founding the company, through work environments and private relationships. The idea for BikerSOS was based on our personal experience, as two of three founders are motorcyclists and know how important safety is due to the dangerous nature of the hobby.

FINANCING

The company is financed by founders' money and investors. BikerSOS works together with a private investor and we have partnerships with major companies working in the motorcycle industry. Projects with these companies are related to the future of motorcycling.

MARKET REACH

The app is usable globally, although most customers are from Europe and the United States.

WHY AUSTRIA?

Austria, especially the city of Linz, provides a healthy ecosystem for startup companies. There is a high-quality university, strong availability of support programs, and the city itself has first-rate infrastructure. In an ideal environment, the Austrian government support programs would make funding decisions more transparent and help startups think big from the first day, like they do in the United States.

LEARNING

In the case of app development, BikerSOS focuses on scaling, but we take the phrase "If you fail, fail fast" to heart. It is important to try to find out as quickly as possible if a service or product is valuable.
We would improve efficiency when handling the range of challenges in short windows of time, by being as agile and flexible as possible throughout growth.

COVID-19

Our product did not change due to the COVID-19 crisis.

bikersos.com

BYRD

All-in-one fulfillment solution to sell and ship goods worldwide in the best conditions that takes ecommerce logistics to the next level

FOUNDED	EXPECTED EXIT	INVESTMENT	HQ	SECTOR	EMPLOYEES
2016	3-5 YEARS (TRADE/SALE)	9 MILLION	VIENNA, BERLIN	LOGISTICS	60+

FOUNDER(S)
Petra Dobrocka, Christoph Krofitsch, Alexander Leichter, Sebastian Mach

BIO
byrd is a tech-driven, third-party logistics and fulfillment company that aims to provide a powerful fulfillment solution for ecommerce, empowering online retailers to grow their business and fulfill their potential.

FOUNDING STORY
While studying, Alex came across the idea as he observed the pain points of shipping products that were sold online. Then Christoph and Sebastian joined, who were at the Practical Robotics Institute Austria (PRIA). Petra Dobrocka, who had worked as head of amrketing at Foodora, joined the conversation on several subjects. Since she was looking for a new challenge, she decided to join the team and completed the founding team. The business model changed quite a lot - we tried to continuously adapt our service to customers' needs in order to help them achieve a competitive advantage with advanced shipping options.

FINANCING
We are mainly financed by grants and investors (business angels and venture capitals).

MARKET REACH
Today, we are shipping parcels from Austria, Germany, the UK, France and the Netherlands.

WHY AUSTRIA?
Vienna was once again voted the most livable city this year and will remain forever in our hearts as a founding place. The funding landscape is advantageous for startups and the startup community is still relatively manageable. This makes it easy to network and get support from other founders. Austria is also recommended due to its opportunities for grants and public funding.

LEARNING
As a startup, you act fast and make a lot of mistakes. In our case it was the same, but we wouldn't do anything different today. One story from the early founding days was when we significantly underestimated the order volume of our online shops in the first Christmas season after founding the company, and we had to pack packages at night to send them in time. We learned from this and know that we have to coordinate and plan capacity for peak times in advance.

An ongoing challenge to date is keeping a clear focus and not working on too many different projects at the same time. As a startup you want to try many different things and sometimes you get excited and try to do too many projects at the same time. But at the end of the day you have to decide where you want to go in the long term and focus on the way to get there

COVID-19
Our business model worked particularly well during the coronavirus outbreak. Our broad partner network allowed us to be flexible and act quickly in the difficult times. In general, we are quite optimistic, since, compared to last year, the number of requests received from merchants increased by almost 500%. Also, COVID-19 came as a wake-up call for many established ecommerce brands to re-evaluate their supply chains, which are now more than ever seeking flexible, on-demand fulfillment solutions, like byrd.

getbyrd.com

Carployee

Carployee

CARPLOYEE

The intelligent ride-sharing app for the daily commute that allows companies and businesses to save money, reduce pollution and get rewards

FOUNDED	EXPECTED EXIT	INVESTMENT	HQ	SECTOR	EMPLOYEES
2018	5 YEARS (TRADE/SALE)	0.5 MILLION	LINZ	MOBILITY, HR, CSR	10

FOUNDER(S)

Gernot Panholzer, Albert Vogl-Bader, Moritz Winko

BIO

Carployee provides companies and employees with the most technologically advanced ridesharing app. We leverage multi-modal ride matching with behavioral economics and measurable impact dimensions.

FOUNDING STORY

The founders come from a rural area in Upper Austria where traffic jams for working commuters are an everyday challenge. After evaluating why traffic jams occur, we focused on the inefficiency of driving cars. Studies reveal that 9 of 10 people drive alone with no passengers at all. However, it is possible to reduce the number of cars by more than 50%, particularly during rush hour. Carployee provides companies and employees with a technologically advanced ridesharing app. We leverage multimodel ride matched with behavioral economics and measurable impact dimensions. The combination of intelligent matching technology, user incentives and environmental tangibility reduces costs on infrastructure, increases employee satisfaction and reduces the organizational CO2 footprint.

FINANCING

Initially, we were bootstrapping and using founders' money. Since then, we have received public grants from the Austrian Research Promotion Agency (FFG) and the Vienna Business Agency, and have secured angel investment. We have a B2B business model that leads to close partnership with corporates, who pay set-up and licensing fees to ensure their employees have the opportunity to use the app. We are collaborating with global HR consultant Mercer for generating employee incentives, Austrian Federal Railways (ÖBB) and Z_GIS - Interfaculty Department of Geoinformatics (University of Salzburg) for mobility behavior, and akaryon for CO2 emission and CSR reporting standards.

MARKET REACH

We are currently active in Austria, Germany and Switzerland. Target markets include Scandinavia, the UK and South Korea. Justifications for target markets include high market demand for carpooling, amount and quality of public mobility initiatives, mobility behavior of commuters in their working environment, and the slight language barrier in Scandinavia and the UK.

WHY AUSTRIA?

There is a variety of advantages for startups founding in Austria. For instance, there is easy access to the ecosystem, including all relevant stakeholders (investors, venture capitals, grants, incubators, accelerators, other startups and more). Austria also has a great public grants system that particularly applies to early-stage startups. Costs of employment, apart from taxes, are rather low compared to other major startup hubs. Access to relevant industry knowhow and skilled employees are also positive aspects.

Austria could improve its startup community by affording easier access to local and international growth capital in higher ranges (Series A+, etc.).

LEARNING

If we could start over again, we would first create a network of experts in the relevant sector. We would also set a preseed strategy with clear focus on value proposition. Furthermore, we would be more aware of the long-term impact of our founding cap table and set it up more efficiently. We have learned how vital it is to connect with other innovators to scale impact globally - by knowledge inclusion.

COVID-19

During the COVID-19 outbreak, we took the opportunity to grow stronger as a team and develop our product further. We stay in close contact with customers and partners, receiving feedback on market developments. Due to the crisis, ourr expansion slowed because of social distancing measures.

carployee.com

SUPPORTED BY
go international
Federal Ministry Republic of Austria Digital and Economic Affairs
WKO

“Not only will you be green and sustainable on the road, but you will also save money.”

GREENSTORM MOBILITY

Europe's largest e-bike marketplace, helping the world become a greener place with refurbished, high-quality, secondhand e-bikes at the best prices

FOUNDED	EXPECTED EXIT	INVESTMENT	HQ	SECTOR	EMPLOYEES
2016	TRADE/SALE	HIGH DOUBLE-DIGIT MILLIONS	KUFSTEIN	e-MOBILITY	100

FOUNDER(S)

Richard Hirschhuber, Wolfgang Spieler, Philipp Zimmermann

BIO

Greenstorm makes the world greener by offering refurbished, high quality, secondhand e-bikes at competitive prices, serviced by trained technicians and brought up to top condition before they can be bought at a preferential price. Our product allows you to be green and sustainable on the road, while saving money. We also provide local hotels with e-bikes in exchange for empty room contingents. After a cycling season, we take back the top e-bikes, service them and offer them for sale.

FOUNDING STORY

The founder was a hotelier back in the day. Three years ago, when he handed over his house, the Auracher Löchl in Kufstein, to the new owners, he met Phillip Zimmermann - his current son-in-law and second managing director. The idea for Greenstorm came from my father, Wolfgang, who started out with 100 e-bikes: if a guest books in a conventional way, he pays 100% of the room price, but if he buys one of the vouchers from the hoteliers on greenstormhotels.com, the hotelier pays half per night.

FINANCING

Greenstorm has long-term investors and it is also financed through deposits by the founders. We have a car leasing cooperation with Sixt and it is currently expanding its network of electric charging stations.

MARKET REACH

Due to the coronavirus situation, we now only focus on the core markets of Germany, Austria and South Tyrol. We have withdrawn from Spain, Belgium, France, Portugal, the Netherlands and Switzerland.

WHY AUSTRIA?

An essential point for a foundation in Austria is the central location in Europe. It offers us good security and a good starting position for our innovative business model. Unfortunately, e-bikes are not included in the *de minimis* support program.

LEARNING

Everything that has been created around Greenstorm in the last years has also been a process of development: As a business grows fast, it is difficult to retain contacts and customers from its early-stage founding period.

COVID-19

On the one hand, we have benefited from the crisis, but on the other hand, it has hit us very hard. Considering the e-bike boom that was triggered, we must play our cards close to our chest. Due to the limited tourism market incurred because of COVID-19, we sell fewer hotel vouchers. Additionally, we have deleted the word "growth" from our vocabulary, at least for the time being - we are now only concentrating on our core markets in Germany, Austria and South Tyrol.

greenstorm.eu

SUPPORTED BY

go international

Federal Ministry Republic of Austria Digital and Economic Affairs

WKO

"It is important to focus on constant execution by breaking down the vision into reachable, small steps."

NEOOM GROUP

Neeom group develops sustainable business models based on renewable energy and creates real added value for customers over generations

FOUNDED	EXPECTED EXIT	INVESTMENT	HQ	SECTOR	EMPLOYEES
2014	5 YEARS (IPO)	5.4 MILLION	FREISTADT	CLEANTECH	41

FOUNDER(S)

Walter Kreisel

BIO

The neoom product family possesses perfectly matched products for the generation, storage and distribution of energy. Neoom relies on the highest quality industrial components and impresses with top design, maximum modularity and best price/performance ratio.

FOUNDING STORY

Neoom group was founded to boost the energy transition with products and software made in Austria. Walter was the single founder in charge of starting the company. Prior to neoom, Walter was working on HOMETEC, which was a system integrator for tailor-made smart home solutions for luxury real estates. Throughout the roughly 300 projects Walter did with his team, he discovered that business logic is only based on individual on-site programing and hardware solutions that are more hobbyist solutions than professional products. With this problem in mind, the only solution for boosting the energy transition was to create high-quality, standardized and scalable products and software. *Voila.* Neoom® (hardware) and NTUITY® (software) were born.

FINANCING

We have financed our venture with founder money, initial investments from two business angels and a subsequent seed funding round with excellent entrepreneurs in Austria. We love to work together with corporate partners on innovation projects that leverage their R&D to create scalable products in order to solve their customers' problems on a massive scale. In terms of investment, we are very selective, only searching for the best-fitting investors, who can help us with know-how, funds and connections to bring the neoom group to a new level.

MARKET REACH

As of 2020, neoom is mainly active in Austria and, to a smaller extent, in Germany, Switzerland and South Tyrol. We did a large project in Kazakhstan, but this was an exception. From Q4/2020 onward, our strategic plan is to enter the German and Swiss markets in a more structured approach with our subsidiaries. Furthermore, an international joint venture outside of the DACH region is planned for 2021.

WHY AUSTRIA?

The benefits of founding the company in Austria and especially Upper Austria are: being surrounded by highly innovative companies that are not only potential clients, but also partners in several strategic projects. This helped us gain traction and link with important contacts; being in close proximity to other important markets such as Germany, Switzerland, Czech Republic and Italy, enabled us efficiently go-to-market in Europe; having an exhaustive selection of grants and subsidies for young entrepreneurs and companies. What it is missing a little bit is the risk appetite from DACH investors to deep dive with young companies in cool visions.

LEARNING

Two things that we would like to be a little bit different are: Maintain laser focus on the three to five topics that leverage the current phase of the company the most and start very early with meeting potential key hires rather than having a condensed and stressed-out recruiting process. It is important to focus on constant execution by breaking down the vision into reachable, small steps.

COVID-19

There were no dramatic changes to our business model through the COVID-19 crisis. We adapted some internal processes to enable more flexibility for remote work and home office and also shifted some external processes from physical to digital channels (e.g. training for their customers via online webinars, etc.). We are lucky our industry (cleantech) benefits from the strong governmental subsidies.

neoom.group

“Our products are already in use throughout Europe and North America.”

SWARM ANALYTICS

Revolutionary AI technology for transforming cameras into smart sensors

FOUNDED	EXPECTED EXIT	INVESTMENT	HQ	SECTOR	EMPLOYEES
2018	N/A	1 MILLION	INNSBRUCK	COMPUTER VISION	12

FOUNDER(S)

Michael Bredehorn, Georg Westner

BIO

Swarm Analytics is able to extract real-time information from video streams directly at their source with unparalleled efficiency. Turning simple cameras into GDPR-compliant smart sensors leads to smarter, faster, easier and trustworthy solutions while increasing affordability. Objects can be detected, classified and followed providing insights without collecting personal data. Based on Swarm Analytics' sensor technology, the solution partners deliver a broad range of end-to-end smart city solutions for traffic, parking, public transport and retail.

FOUNDING STORY

Founded in 2018 in Innsbruck while studying at university together. Our products are already in use throughout Europe and North America. They are available as ready-to-use edge hardware and as virtual software packages.

FINANCING

Swarm Analytics is financed through investors, grants and revenue.

MARKET REACH

Our main focus at the moment is Europe. So far, we have sold to over 10 countries, including the United States. We have contracts with Original Equipment Manufacturer (OEM) partners and system integrators.

WHY AUSTRIA?

Bureaucracy for startup companies is something we would like to see improved.

COVID-19

There were no strategic changes due to COVID-19 but there were tactical ones. We were negatively affected as there was a period of increased uncertainty. Some customers closed and were not able to invest in Swarm Analytics' solutions.

swarm-analytics.com

“Tractive’s mission is to strengthen the bond between pets and their owners by leveraging technology to ensure a healthier, longer and safer life together.”

TRACTIVE

Pet wearables, apps and online services, providing pet owners and pet lovers alike with more happiness, security, and peace of mind

FOUNDED	EXPECTED EXIT	INVESTMENT	HQ	SECTOR	EMPLOYEES
2012	N/A	N/A	PASCHING	PETTECH	100

FOUNDER(S)
Michael Hurnaus, Michael Lettner, Michael Tschernuth

BIO
Tractive is a GPS technology for tracking the whereabouts of your cats and dogs that is linked to a free smartphone app. Tractive's mission is to strengthen the bond between pets and their owners by leveraging technology to ensure a healthier, longer and safer life together.

FOUNDING STORY
The founding team was connected by a mutual friend who knew each founder well and knew that this would be a well-matched team. A friend's dog was lost in early 2012 in the US. I was part of the search crew. Luckily, they found the escape artist about an hour later. After that, they were all surprised that there was not a single product on the market that helped people find their dogs using their smartphones.

tractive.com

FINANCING
Tractive is supported by AWS and FFG grants, founder money, as well as some very early business angels, including Hansi Hansmann. In the past we have seen that many large corporations simply move too slowly for a fast-paced startup or scaleup. We avoid partnerships unless we will be working with a division of a corporate that is independent and has decision-making power on certain topics, so we can act fast. If a partnership requires a legal document that is more than two pages, we typically politely decline. This has served us well in the past.

MARKET REACH
Tractive is available worldwide, but strongly focuses on Europe, US, Canada and Australia for the time being.

WHY AUSTRIA?
Government grants and early-stage support are certainly helpful for companies based in Austria. Also, the political landscape is fairly stable and the ecosystem for (early-stage) investors is growing. On other fronts, such as taxation, we would prefer more flexible forms of corporations (GmbH-light) and looser regulations and sandboxes for startups. There are certainly areas for improvements to re-create Austria's reputation as an interesting market for international startups. Ways Austria could improve its startup ecosystem include a more effienct tax regime to allow employees to participate in the growth and success of the company (employee stock ownership plan or PSP).

LEARNING
We would do many things the exact same way. Alternatively, we would likely hire more senior talent earlier in the game to save time addressing many challenges we had along the way. Startup life is like a rollercoaster, a steep one, at times. As the startup was growing, we learned that, at times, things did not go so well, but learned that it is important to stay calm, think clearly and eventually everything will normalize.

COVID-19
Tractive was slightly impacted regarding the quantity of device sales during the lockdown. Amazon only sold essential goods in certain countries for a few weeks, which did not include Tractive GPS trackers. However, Tractive recovered quickly and exeperienced several record months. Overall, the impact was slightly negative or neutral.

FOR SALE
FOR SALE

PROPTECH & AGTECH

Only 2.6% of startups in Austria consider themselves connected to the real estate industry, according to the Austrian Startup Monitor 2019. However, investment in the property technology sector has been bountiful, with several double-digit million rounds for PropTech startups in 2020 alone. Austria's market in agriculture technology is rather small, yet very interesting and active. A number of promising seed investments were made in 2019 and 2020 and the Austrian and EU governments provide many subsidies and grants for the agriculture sectors.

BIMSPOT

A disruptive technology for data and model-driven decision making for building information modeling (BIM)

FOUNDED	EXPECTED EXIT	INVESTMENT	HQ	SECTOR	EMPLOYEES
2018	3-6 YEARS (MERGER, TRADE/SALE, MBO, IPO)	N/A	VIENNA	REAL ESTATE/ PROPTECH	15

FOUNDER(S)

Christoph Degendorfer

BIO

Bimspot was founded with the aim of unleashing the full potential of building information modeling (BIM) projects. For the first time, digital models of a building can be developed independent of individual choice of software. It is life cycle-oriented and with clear responsibilities of all stakeholders. Bimspot brings transparency and ensures quality and efficiency while planning, constructing and operating a building.

FOUNDING STORY

The founders knew one another prior to founding. One of us was working as an architect on a project using building information modeling (BIM) and after that, he co-founded a consulting company focused on BIM.

FINANCING

The company is financed through grants, business angels, and venture capital. We were also in an accelerator program provided by Drees & Sommer in Stuttgart.

MARKET REACH

We have users in 70 countries spread all over the world. The best markets in which BIM/Digitalisation are already further developed include the United Kingdom, Nordics, BeNeLux, Brazil, the United States, Mexico, Australia.

WHY AUSTRIA?

We already had a business network in Austria before creating bimspot. Founding in Austria has the added benefit of wide varieties of public grants. However, we believe that in Austria, a founder's mindset should be better supported and cultivated in academic curriculum.

LEARNING

We learned that there is not one overarching lesson, so much as it is about improving every day as much as possible.

COVID-19

During the lockdown, we did not change the product, but we did evolve our communication methods. On a positive side, it brought a boost for digital products and online workflows; on the negative side, it caused a heavy impact on the industry, making it harder to sell our product.

bimspot.io

SUPPORTED BY

go international

Federal Ministry Republic of Austria Digital and Economic Affairs

WKO

W48
STARTUP LOFTS

iDWELL

The first SaaS CRM software in the property management market that integrates all communication channels to one platform

FOUNDED	EXPECTED EXIT	INVESTMENT	HQ	SECTOR	EMPLOYEES
2017	4 YEARS (TRADE/SALE, IPO)	1 MILLION	VIENNA	PROPTECH	25

FOUNDER(S)

Alexander Roth

BIO

iDWELL is mobile consumer relationship management software specifically designed for real estate management. It enables the automation of routine processes and reduces all communication between the parties involved in property management.

FOUNDING STORY

I worked for BlackFridaySale in the UK, a well-known ecommerce platform that hosts an annual Black Friday sale event. During my time with this ecommerce company, I decided to found my own business within the PropTech sector, iDWELL, together with some of my team members from BlackFridaySale. My father-in-law, a property management agent, constantly received calls and texts from tenants regarding issues or damages in his properties. I started to wonder why my father-in-law would take calls from his customers outside of business hours if their issues did not require immediate fixing. He conducted some market research and found out that there was no real digital solution on the market enabling easy 24/7 communication between property management companies, tenants and landlords.

FINANCING

The company is mostly financed through investors; additionally, we managed to secure a grant from the Vienna Business Agency for our AI project. Being financed by investors gives us the advantage to have access to experienced industry experts. On the partner side, we work with enterprise resource planning and hardware corporations. Together it enables us to combine and integrate our softwares to deliver the best possible experience to customers of both companies.

MARKET REACH

At the moment our focus is on Austria and Germany, as they are relatively similar markets and share the same language. This makes the expansion in both countries easy and efficient. In Austria and Germany, we manage around 350,000 apartment units. Until the end of 2020, we plan to increase the number of units to 750,000.

WHY AUSTRIA?

Austria offers many benefits to founders, such as its relatively easy process for founding a company and its subsidy benefits. However, the most significant advantage of Austria is its location in Central Europe, even for a company like iDWELL,which, as a young SaaS software, does most of its business online. Austria's location provides two main benefits: On one hand, to work in an industry with highly traditional core values, the real estate business, in which most business partners value and expect personal contact. On the other hand, the location allows them to quickly scale their company. A hurdle for startups in Austria would definitely be the high tax on employees. This makes you think twice before hiring another full-time employee.

LEARNING

Starting over, we would hire senior and the right sales people from the start, who are able to sell our product and the world to our clients. We have learned to frequently communicate to our team the reasons behind establishing this startup.

COVID-19

The real estate business is still very traditional and, as an industry, has one of the lowest digitalization rates in the world. We like to say that our biggest competitor is still Excel. During the COVID-19 lockdown, we saw a huge surge in interest in our SaaS software, as real estate companies quickly recognized the need to implement digital channels to communicate with both their customers and their employees working from home. We took advantage of this opportunity and made it easier and with less burden to implement iDWELL. Even now, after the lockdown, we benefit from the effects COVID-19 on the entire real estate industry, as many companies realize now what digitalization offers benefits, such as increased efficiency, lower costs and higher customer satisfaction.

idwell.at

SUPPORTED BY

go international

Federal Ministry Republic of Austria Digital and Economic Affairs

WKO

“Success is always a result of focused, hard work.”

MYACKER

MyAcker offers online garden parcels directly operated by its users with real harvest no matter where they live

FOUNDED	EXPECTED EXIT	INVESTMENT	HQ	SECTOR	EMPLOYEES
2018	6 YEARS (MERGER)	150,000	SPITTAL	DIGITALIZATION	8

FOUNDER(S)
Christoph Raunig, Patrick Kleinfercher

BIO
MyAcker is a "digital gardening" solution that keeps its customers involved in every step of the way. It allows its users to run their own garden parcels with an individual choice of organic seeds and plants, and with the responsibility to check on the conditions of their vegetables and herbs growing in myAcker's fields within their online accounts. Ripe vegetables are shipped with a sustainable, CO2 neutral service. Full transparency throughout the entire process is essential.

FOUNDING STORY
The founders gained experience in different industries and met by chance in December 2016, when Christoph had the idea for this unique online gardening system. Patrick was enthusiastic about this concept and suggested to turn this idea into action and to use his own fields to grow the vegetables. The idea was developed when we were students at University in Salzburg, where just a few people have enough space to cultivate their own vegetables.

FINANCING
Until the proof of concept and proof market phase, myAcker was completely financed by the founders' money. The roll out process was supported by an Austrian business angel.

MARKET REACH
There are some markets like Belgium, Netherlands or the Czech Republic, where potential partners are already interested starting a business using myAcker's model.

WHY AUSTRIA?
One of the best aspects of founding a company in Austrias is the country's size and the infrastructure. Especially when shipping products, this allows us to reach every corner of Austria overnight.

LEARNING
The primary lesson is that success is always a result of focused, hard work.

COVID-19
MyAcker was affected extremely positively by COVID-19. All gardens for 2020 have been sold before the official start of the season. Additionally, there is a waiting list for 2021 with 280 reservations.

myacker.com

"PlanRadar's customers manage over 25,000 projects per week in over 45 countries worldwide."

PLANRADAR

Project management solutions for construction and real estate

FOUNDED	EXPECTED EXIT	INVESTMENT	HQ	SECTOR	EMPLOYEES
2014	N/A	33 MILLION	VIENNA	PROPTECH	140

FOUNDER(S)

Domagoj Dolinsek, Clemens Hammerl, Ibrahim Imam, Constantin Köck, Sander van de Rijdt

BIO

PlanRadar enables digital documentation and communication for construction and real estate projects, including easy ticketing, automatic notifications and digital overview of blueprints.

FOUNDING STORY

In 2013, I had the idea to create a technological solution to resolve the complex challenges of construction management. Together with two experts in software development, we created the Beta version of PlanRadar. Once the initial technical development was done, the product caught the attention of Sander van de Rijdt and Ibrahim Imam, two young entrepreneurs. They completed the founding team and became Co-CEOs, taking over daily operations and developing the strategic orientation of the company. With more than 10 years of experience in the planning and construction management of large projects, we have a deep understanding of the challenges and requirements our customers are facing.

FINANCING

We financed the earliest stage ourselves with the help of cashflow. However, we were quickly in a position to provide a product with a clear USP and outstanding growth rates. That caught the attention of international investors like Insight Partners, Cavalry Ventures and e.ventures, who support our strategy for global growth.

MARKET REACH

PlanRadar's customers manage over 25,000 projects per week in over 45 countries worldwide. Our strategy is to be internationally known, but locally present in all our core markets. As a result, we now have offices in London, Zagreb for the SEE region, Stockholm for the Nordics, Paris, Moscow and Warsaw. We are planning to open entities in Milan, Madrid, Amsterdam and Bucharest. We might expand to the UAE and Australia, but it will depend on the overall economic situation. We carefully watch and analyze the needs of our industry all over the world and have identified these markets as "easy wins."

WHY AUSTRIA?

Strategically, Vienna is the ideal hub for PlanRadar's business. The high standard of living attracts talent from all over the world, making recruiting in headquarters easier. The construction and real estate industries in the DACH region are well-respected overseas, so our success here has also laid the groundwork for our international expansion.

LEARNING

At this stage, the PlanRadar team would not do anything differently, considering there are always challenges when building a company. Our lessons took place over three stages. (1) From bootstrapping to startup, it was important to build a team around an idea and the MVP; doing proofs of concept and finding the first customers. (2) From the stage of startup to a company, important elements included proof of market, bringing in middle management and developing the organizational design. (3) From company to scaleup, we focused on growth, bringing in additional departments like CS, legal, and others; having 100+ employees and €10 million+ revenue.

COVID-19

Considering we provide a digital product, we have had it easier than other industries, and the COVID-19 crisis even pushed our growth in some aspects. However, missing out on opportunities to attend exhibitions and trade fairs and the chance to meet potential clients in person are losses. We changed how we reach out to customers, developing webinars on industry-relevant topics, and we will continue to do this beyond the end of the COVID-19 crisis as it has proved to be very successful.

planradar.com

SUPPORTED BY

go international

Federal Ministry Republic of Austria Digital and Economic Affairs

WKO

“Our goal was to digitalize analog, sluggish processes for special requests for flats, houses and offices.”

PROPSTER

Propster provides solutions for real estate configuration processing, online sampling, apartment handover and defect management

FOUNDED	EXPECTED EXIT	INVESTMENT	HQ	SECTOR	EMPLOYEES
2017	7 YEARS (IPO)	0.75 MILLION	VIENNA	PROPTECH	25

FOUNDER(S)
Milan Zahradnik, Klaus Kainrad

BIO
Propster's goal is to convert the entire communication and organizational process between the apartment buyer and the property developer or project developer.

FOUNDING STORY
Milan, founder and CEO, worked in a marketing and communication agency with a focus on real estate for 15 years, as has co-founder Klaus. We always listened carefully to our clients. Our goal was always to push digitalization, i.e. to digitalize analog, sluggish processes for special requests for flats, houses and offices. With our platform, we have managed to significantly reduce the amount of time required and, in addition, we help real estate companies generate additional income with our projects and to create a better buying experience in order to increase the satisfaction of the buyers.

FINANCING
The company is financed by founder money and money from four business angels. Furthermore, we have been generating turnover from our customers since the beginning.

MARKET REACH
We are active in Austria, Germany, Switzerland and Slovenia. Our next target market is the United Kingdom. In the course of our Pi-Labs Accelerator (VC from London), we were able to establish many valuable contacts there. Furthermore, we found out that our product has found fertile ground there.

WHY AUSTRIA?
First of all, Vienna is our hometown. Due to the construction industry, there is an enormous potential of customers from the real estate industry for us to work with. Austria's location in the center of Europe is also a positive factor for a foundation in Austria. Austria offers a very good infrastructure for proptech startups.

LEARNING
We built up a good team from the very beginning and our customer base is constantly growing. It all comes as it must when you put all your positive energy into the project. Of course, there are some things that could be done faster or better, but that is not worth mentioning. We have learned that the needs of our customers are not the same in every country. Other countries have different customs, so to speak.

COVID-19
With our collaboration and consumer platform, we enable real estate companies to configure properties based on our project criteria and offer their customers, such as buyers, tenants and investors, a suitable selection of products and services for their flats, houses or offices, a service which is handled digitally. COVID-19 only had a limited and short-term effect on us when the work on construction sites was stopped for a few weeks. With the expansion of our platform and the addition of various digital services, we were even able to take advantage of this.

propster.tech

SUPPORTED BY
go international
Federal Ministry Republic of Austria Digital and Economic Affairs
WKO

SMAXTEC

Early detection for health, reproduction and nutrition for cows to avoid infection and address symptoms early on

FOUNDED	EXPECTED EXIT	INVESTMENT	HQ	SECTOR	EMPLOYEES
2009	4 YEARS (TRADE/SALE)	6.5 MILLION	GRAZ	AGTECH	50

FOUNDER(S)
Stefan Rosenkranz, Mario Fallast

BIO
smaXtec is a revolutionary solution in a traditional sector, helping farmers to better understand their cows. With smaXtec, dairy farmers have a unique and secure system at their hand, setting a new standard in early detection in the areas of animal health, reproduction and feeding management.

FOUNDING STORY
The two engineers and founders recognized that it was not possible to continuously and automatically monitor essential vital parameters of dairy cows. Through networking and cooperation with the Research Institute Raumberg-Gumpenstein, we were able to find a practical solution to the problem that can be applied on commercial dairy farms of all sizes. Research and development resulted in a market-ready product. The idea came out of research, when it became clear that continuous monitoring of vital parameters inside the rumen was not yet possible. The goal was to make important health parameters of cows measurable continuously and automatically.

FINANCING
The company is financed from grants, founder money and by investors.

MARKET REACH
Currently, the product is sold in 25 countries around the world. After the establishment of subsidiaries in Germany and England, the next goal will be to enter the US market.

WHY AUSTRIA?
Graz is an attractive business location because of the expertise and knowledge both from a technical and agricultural point of view. Another advantage of funding in Austria is the central location in Europe. Furthermore, the company benefited from organizations supporting startups, e.g. the startup incubator Science Park in Graz with the unique knowledge, its mentors and access to a broad network. In order to become a successful startup, it would help local entrepreneurs to have more venture capital available, especially at the time of shifting the focus from product development toward sales.

LEARNING
With hindsight, we would certainly approach some challenges we faced differently. At all times, we tried to make decisions according to the current state of knowledge. During the expansion of the company, the biggest challenge certainly was to make investment decisions at the right time. An additional critical challenge was to recruit qualified and suitable staff for all important areas as quickly as possible.

COVID-19
COVID-19 did not impact the company negatively. However, we began to use more digital solutions due to the restrictions, e.g. for online consultancy and sales.

smaxtec.com

SUPPORTED BY

go international

Federal Ministry Republic of Austria Digital and Economic Affairs

WKO

“Low investment costs, rapid amortization and agile scaling options create Storebox’s proven advantage.”

STOREBOX

Storebox is the first fully digitized self-storage solution in Europe

FOUNDED	EXPECTED EXIT	INVESTMENT	HQ	SECTOR	EMPLOYEES
2016	TRADE/SALE	8 MILLION	VIENNA	LOGISTICS & PROPTECH	40

FOUNDER(S)

Johannes Braith, Ferdinand Dietrich, Christoph Sandraschitz

BIO

Storebox has 60 self-storage locations in central Vienna and offers you storage space in your neighborhood. The entire process from compartment selection to booking is handled online via the website and via a mobile application. This allows immediate access to the storage compartment right after booking - allowing also for easy access in the evenings or weekends. Thanks to the innovative access system, Storebox can be accessed around the clock. Smart sensors measure temperature, humidity and access activity in real time. Storebox is video-monitored and stored items are insured. As a franchise partner, you benefit from a proven concept and an established brand. Low investment costs, rapid amortization and agile scaling options create Storebox's proven advantage.

FOUNDING STORY

The founders were friends in Vienna and the idea was sparked from an instance in which the CEO's 80-year-old neighbour was renting her cellar to a tradesman for storage.

FINANCING

Storebox was started with founders' money, business angels and venture capital. SIGNA is a partner company.

MARKET REACH

We are currently operating in Austria, Germany and Switzerland, and will target the BeNeLux region next.

WHY AUSTRIA?

We chose starting up in Austria due to the availability of grants, good access to seed money and availability of talent in-country. Austria could provide better access to money for later-stage startups, including Series A, B and C investment rounds.

LEARNING

The Storebox team learned the importance of taking our time to develop company structure and culture. Looking back, we would think bigger and raise more money in the early stage.

COVID-19

Storebox did not experience a major pivot in response to COVID-19. Storebox was positively affected in terms of consumer business, but negatively affected in terms of planned fundraising activities.

yourstorebox.com

NEWS

ENTERPRISE, B2B & SAAS

A staggering 36% of startups only do business with companies (B2B) and another 24% make the majority of their revenue from B2B sales. From enterprise communication and social media tools to cybersecurity and analytics for restaurants, Austrian solutions for the workplace and infrastructure are far-reaching and cutting edge. Currently, 15.3% of companies operate in this sector, according to the Austrian Startup Monitor 2019.

"A loyal and trustworthy team is key."

FOODNOTIFY

A modern and easy-to-use inventory management system for the gastronomy and hotel industries

FOUNDED	EXPECTED EXIT	INVESTMENT	HQ	SECTOR	EMPLOYEES
2014	2-3 YEARS (MERGER, TRADE/SALE, MBO)	4 MILLION	VIENNA	SAAS FOR HOSPITALITY	18

FOUNDER(S)

Adnan Hanic, Mirza Muharemagic, Christina Primus, Thomas Primus

BIO

FoodNotify is a progressive enterprise resource planning (ERP) platform for gastronomy and hotel industries. It allows you to connect, synchronize and automate most goods-related processes in your company, from inventory management and procurement to recipe management and controlling.

FOUNDING STORY

Thomas' dream was bringing more transparency to the food sector. With his idea in mind he met Mirza and Adnan. In the following months discussions about the idea deepened and Christina joined the team. Working from Vienna and Sarajevo, we built our first minimum viable product. Passion is a common ground that unites the four founders. Everyone is very passionate about what they do and that is essential for starting up a company.

FINANCING

The founders bootstrapped FoodNotify with the support of grants and startup programs until 2017. After, we decided to work with a strategic investment partner. We generated revenues from the very first moment we went online with our product. Simultaneously, we won client projects, which helped us generate revenues and develop our main product. Over time, we identified different income streams and refined our target groups.

MARKET REACH

We are active in Germany, Austria and Switzerland. Our customers are gastronomy and hotel enterprises that have a minimum of 3 locations, such as chains or franchises. We are expanding in alignment with the locations of our customers and partners. We won 2020's "go-international" program for Silicon Valley, but due to coronavirus, we were unable to travel to the United States; however, we connected with market players there.

WHY AUSTRIA?

The Austrian market and its participants afford a critical and challenging environment for product innovation. This means you can introduce your product and receive constructive feedback. The expectations and requirements are high, and we were able to adapt our product in order to scale up. Furthermore, the Austrian government established a convenient startup environment and possibilities to found more easily, have access to money and be a part of the presence of a growing investment scene. In our point of view, it is essential for an economy to support young entrepreneurs and push innovation. One difficulty of operating in Austria is the high taxes compared to other markets.

LEARNING

We created a product from scratch without knowing the market and the target group with its demands and requirements, which was beneficial to bringing a new view to the industry. As we developed the first prototype, we talked to insiders and customers. What we missed was the opportunity to examine our target group more closely, leading to product changes later on. A motivated and loyal team is important for moving things forward if they are open, challenge each other every day and leveraging the power of groups is key.

COVID-19

The COVID-19 crisis affected our business positively, as it increased digitalization in the hospitality industry. Our target clients recognize that digitalization is key for survival. Therefore, FoodNotify receives many requests for consulting. We adapted our communication, engaged in more marketing activities, and wrote articles and e-books about how to digitalize a restaurant or hotel chain.

foodnotify.com

“We have learned how to focus and evaluate properly, and how to sell in Europe.”

GRAPE

A software solution providing secure video, voice and text conversations that happen inside your favorite business tools

FOUNDED	EXPECTED EXIT	INVESTMENT	HQ	SECTOR	EMPLOYEES
2014	SALE/IPO	3 MILLION	VIENNA	COMMUNICATION	20

FOUNDERS

Felix Häusler (CEO), Stefan Kröner (CTO)

BIO

Grape is the result of an extensive R&D project aimed at improving corporate communication.

FOUNDING STORY

The founding team knew each other from previous projects. We had a little agency called UberGrape that built web products for customers. During that time we stumbled upon the McKinsey's Global Economy study, that showed that 61% of all office time is wasted on collaboration and communication.
We wanted to change this, so we started to investigate how communication could put the human more front and center.
The rest is history.

FINANCING

Very early on, our team received a research grant from the FFG , which allowed the team to collaborate with the Austrian Research Institute for Artificial Intelligence, to understand and improve human communication with modern technology. The prototype was enough to convince Josh Miller (Creative Labs at Facebook), Betaworks (Twitter, Pinterest, etc.) to invest in us, allowing us to launch what is now known as Grape.
At the moment, we are mostly looking for strategic investors that can help us grow beyond Europe.

MARKET REACH

We are currently active in the DACH region, Poland, UK, the Nordics, and South Africa. We plan to expand our reach to the rest of the EU.

WHY AUSTRIA?

Austria was chosen for its high living standards, peace and stability, a lot of tech universities, and for being located in the center of Europe. When it comes to Austrian startup regulations, we hope for more tax benefits for startup investment and we think that an international format (Ltd.) could also help - but we've heard that's on the way.

LEARNING

A narrower focus, both on the product and market side helps a lot with growth. It's like achieving lightspeed: The less you weigh, the less energy you need to reach high velocity. Also, there is no special hockey-stick growth, it's all a lie. Growth takes effort and you need to allocate at least 50% of your spending to it, no matter how cool your product is.

COVID-19

Of course, there are some positive economic effects of the current COVID crisis. But on the other hand, the market is transforming quickly and we would have loved to have a bit more cash to advertise during this wave of digitalisation. We also miss hanging out at the office a lot, but under the current circumstances it looks like we will be working from home until the second half of 2021.

grape.io

“A good team beats everything!”

HELLO AGAIN

Pioneers in digitalization creating new opportunities for companies to build stronger customer loyalty

FOUNDED	EXPECTED EXIT	INVESTMENT	HQ	SECTOR	EMPLOYEES
2017	N/A	<1 MILLION	LINZ	CUSTOMER LOYALTY	40

FOUNDERS
Sebastian Auberger (CIO), Mario Pecile (CSO), Michael Schöndorfer (CTO), Franz Tretter (CEO).

BIO
Hello again supports companies with the use of intelligent digital technologies to leverage their individual customer loyalty in order to build personal communication with their clients.

FOUNDING STORY
The founders met through business and private networks. We realized that many clubs and discos invest a lot of time and money into to build their community on social media platforms such as Facebook or Instagram. With the effect that they have to pay to reach their audience afterward. Additionally we recognized that customer loyalty would become more important because Gen Y is not as loyal to brands as the previous generation used to be. As such, we had the idea to build a brand community for each company, using social media as a multiplier. Since smartphones are the preferred medium in society, we built a loyalty club program as an app for mobile phones. During the first stage resulted in 70 clubs in Austria, then for small and middle business in 10 countries.

FINANCING
The first three years were bootstrapped. For our rollout in Germany we took an investment (higher, 6-digit figure) from investors such as Alexander Kudlich, Florian Gschwandtner, and Hansi Hansmann. We started a sales partnership with one of Austria's largest corporations, the Österreichische Post. We have cooperations with Müller, Sport2000 and Maxi Cosy, who are using our loyalty solution in various countries.

MARKET REACH
Our loyalty solution is used in 10 countries. We started in Austria, where we are ranked No. 2 in the loyalty market (JÖ Bonusclub). More than 300 companies trust in hello again. Currently, we are focusing on the DACH region (Germany, Austria, Switzerland) to grow to 1,000 clients, because of the language, similar market and distance.

WHY AUSTRIA?
Austria is attractive for its high standard of living, solid social system, strong personal networks and high density of small and midsized businesses. To support these, we will have to build the most modern and easy-to-use loyalty solutions.

LEARNING
A good team beats everything!

COVID-19
Due to COVID-19, digitalization for small and mid-size businesses, and these companies are now more aware of customer loyalty than ever. This change affected our company positively.

helloagain.at

MYPRIVACY

An easy-to-use mobile privacy toolbox that will help you protect your personal information on your device and around the web

FOUNDED	EXPECTED EXIT	INVESTMENT	HQ	SECTOR	EMPLOYEES
2018	5 YEARS (TRADE/SALE)	0.8 MILLION	VIENNA	CYBERSECURITY	8

FOUNDERS

Christoph Drescher, Erwin Toplak

BIO

Benefiting from years of our team's experience in the field of IT, cybersecurity and encryption, we invent, develop and produce innovative data protection products and solutions, for private, business and industry customers - as off-the-shelf and customized turnkey solutions.

FOUNDING STORY

Erwin Toplak, previous board member of Kapsch Traffic Com AG (KTC) and Christoph Drescher met during joint projects in KTC between 2008 and 2014. The idea came after we saw the market need.

FINANCING

The company is financed by founder money, a new strategic investor and grants. At the moment, we are preparing for our first proof of concept.

MARKET REACH

We are active in the DACH region and further expansion will target more countries in Europe.

WHY AUSTRIA?

Austria was chosen for its stable political environment, strong local network and the location of our families in Austria. In the future, we hope the Austrian startup climate provides similar investment schemes and benefits form the UK.

LEARNING

If we could start over, we would acquire more technical experience from the beginning. We have learned to find qualified staff in Austria, and are now hiring outside of Austria due to Austria's lack of deep tech experience.

COVID-19

The crisis did not particularly affect us, since we were still at a stage of fine-tuning our business model and not taking risks.

myprivacy.cc

“We didn’t understand why translations cannot be booked online like a hotel room or a flight.”

NATIVY TRANSLATIONS

3,600 professional translators working with 500 language combinations in 35 areas of exerptise, including legal, finance, engineering, IT and marketing

FOUNDED	EXPECTED EXIT	INVESTMENT	HQ	SECTOR	EMPLOYEES
2011	3 YEARS (MERGER, SALE)	1.2 MILLION	VIENNA	TRANSLATION AND LOCALIZATION	10

FOUNDERS

Josef Brunner, Anchal Lochan

BIO

Nativy is the easiest way for business-to-business clients to commission professional translation, copywriting and SEO services. Our platform allows clients to manage translations on a company-wide level: we can share an order overview with colleagues; use the company-wide translation databse and team of preferred translators; rate translations online and get cumulative invoices. Our clients range form multinational banks and industrial manufacturers to local PR agencies.

FOUNDING STORY

Josef started Nativy in 2011 with Anton. In 2015 it was just myself and a part-time developer who continued working on Nativy. Anton left the company in 2015 due to stagnant growth. For the next few months, Josef ran the company along with a part-time student. In 2016, Anchal joined and took over Sales and Operations. We fixed our most high-priority bugs and focused on funding and hiring new talent. Ever since, our revenue has grown year on year.

FINANCING

Nativy is bootstrapped and the bulk of our operating costs are covered by the revenue we generate. We received several grants from the Austrian Promotional Bank (AWS), the Austrian Research Promotion Agency and Wirtschaftsagentur Wien. On top of this, the founders and three investors each invested five-digit amounts.

MARKET REACH

Most of our revenue comes from Germany, Austria, Switzerland and the United States. Our goal is to continue expanding within our existing markets and we plan to target Scandinavia next.

WHY AUSTRIA?

In our experience the Austrian private sector is open to trying out novel solutions like ours. We already translate for 20 of the Top 100 companies in Austria. The local competition still manages translations manually over email, the way they have been for the past 20 years, and our technology gives us a huge edge over this competition.

LEARNING

It took us seven years to make the first million in gross revenue; 18 months to make the second; and the third is currently in the making. B2B marketplaces are not built overnight—it takes long to establish yourself but if you keep the quality high, clients will stay with you.

COVID-19

We saw an influx of new clients who decided to switch to Nativy for the advantages that our cloud service offers: 24/7 online ordering and department-wide order overviews, where everyone can see the status of all ongoing orders and access past translations. We did not need to avail of any COVID-19-related loans and plan to break even this year.

nativy.com

SUPPORTED BY

go international

Federal Ministry
Republic of Austria
Digital and
Economic Affairs

WKO

"We saw how chaotic the handling of order taking was on the supplier side and how frustrated chefs were."

ORDERLION

All-in-one shop system chosen by over 150 catering suppliers in four countries and more than 30 cities to upgrade their customer relationships

FOUNDED	EXPECTED EXIT	INVESTMENT	HQ	SECTOR	EMPLOYEES
2018	5 YEARS (MERGER, IPO)	1.2 MILLION	VIENNA	B2B SAAS	14

FOUNDERS

Patrick Schubert, Stefan Strohmer

BIO

The company created an industry standard for the digitalization of customer relationships between suppliers and restauranteurs. It is the first shop system optimized for the catering industry - to promote strong customer relationships on a digital level and to improve processes around ordering for suppliers and restaurateurs alike. Today, Orderlion is used by over 150 partner suppliers in four countries and over 2,500 satisfied restaurateurs.

FOUNDING STORY

Right out of university, I founded an IT consulting company developing a broad spectrum of highly specialized software solutions for industrial companies, mainly in the food industry. The idea came out of our consulting business; we saw how chaotic the handling of order-taking was on the supplier side and how frustrated chefs were.

FINANCING

The company is financed through an angel investment round, a seed round with venture capital and two government grants, including the Austrian Research Promotion Agency (FFG) and Austrian promotion bank (AWS).

MARKET REACH

We are currently active in five countries, Austria being the biggest, followed by Germany.

WHY AUSTRIA?

Austria provides convenient access to government grants. Vienna is a great environment for hiring, as international people know it for its great living standards. Therefore, many are willing to relocate. We believe that having more experienced serial founders that can mentor new startup founders through their early days would improve the ecosystem.

LEARNING

We would have expanded the team earlier since it helped us expand our market share and product offering significantly. We also learned to never assume, but always test.

COVID-19

For a short period during lockdown, we expanded our product offering from business-to-business to business-to-consumer so that private households were able to get fresh produce delivered from local wholesalers.

orderlion.com

“We don’t want a collection app, because you can already collect at the jö-club and payback - so why not create a platform that makes it possible for everyone.”

ORDITO SOLUTIONS

A food-ordering solution enabling anyone to use a QR code scan to access restaurant menus and order directly

FOUNDED	EXPECTED EXIT	INVESTMENT	HQ	SECTOR	EMPLOYEES
2019	2 YEARS TRADE/SALE	0	ST POELTEN	GASTROTECH	5

FOUNDERS

Maurice Beurskens, Eric Weisz

BIO

Ordito offers an ordering platform for restaurants. No matter whether in, outside or on the way to the restaurant. With ordito, the customer can order via links or QR codes easily on the web from everywhere.

FOUNDING STORY

The team of founders met at the IMC University of Applied Sciences Krems and got to know another founder via the startup platform brutkasten.

To make a long story short: the founding story involved traveling to Asia, America and skiing. In Asia we observed that people order their food in a restaurant via WeChat; in the US people order their food before they get to the restaurant. We looked at the market and found a fragmented app market. Every restaurant had its own app, or every city had its own provider. We thought "We don't want a collection app, because you can already collect at the jö-club and payback - so why not create a platform that makes it possible for everyone."

FINANCING

Ordito Solutions is still completely boot-strapped, and we were able to keep our cashburn manageable. Therefore, we have not needed any investments until now by leveraging good deals and grants. Ordito Solutions did work with corporations as investors and partners. There were in a lot of promising meetings before COVID-19. Unfortunately, with the crisis these conversa-tions were postponed. Throughout the crisis we began to work with gastronomy and food retailer Kastner, which is located in Zwettl, Lower Austria.

MARKET REACH

We started in Austria as our home market, and are currently in Germany, experiencing more growth each week. We have been in contact with partners from the Netherlands. In these markets our customers, the restaurant owners, but also the users, are more open for technological solutions. The Austrian gastronomy market is a bit conservative and prefers to stick to old ordering methods.

WHY AUSTRIA?

The scene is compact and offers great opportunities for networking, receiving support and quickly finding reliable partners. The country has many talented and motivated young founders, who can rely on a good funding structure. If we had it our way, bureaucracy in Austria would be streamlined and easier to obtain subsidies. Implement the entrepreneurship as a practical subject of study including small startup projects, so that potential founders are less fearful.

LEARNING

There are strong dependencies in the industry that can have strong impacts on product development. Before we would set up a new company, we would carry out more intensive market analysis and test even faster.

COVID-19

At the beginning of COVID-19 we were strongly affected because we developed an ordering solution for in-house service in restaurants. Since restaurants had to close, our product was no longer relevant. However, we quickly adapted to the market and launched an out-of-home version. This allowed customers to order and pick up their food while on the move or have it delivered by caterers. We found a partner during the crisis and were able to offer our service free of charge. In alignment with regulatory requirements of the government, we have developed a guest registration system and now serve more than 100 restaurants.

ordito.at

PRESONO

Software to create unique professional presentations intuitively and quickly and easily manage all tasks in a team

FOUNDED	EXPECTED EXIT	INVESTMENT	HQ	SECTOR	EMPLOYEES
2015	3 YEARS (MERGER, TRADE/SALE, IPO)	2.4 MILLION	LINZ	SAAS	16

FOUNDERS

Hannes Freudenthaler, Margot Helm, Andrea Lehner

BIO

Our startup completely rethinks the subject of presentation and combines professional presentation and perfect management in a revolutionary software solution. presono is the only software provider to have developed a complete solution that professionally covers all elementary areas in one platform, from the design and creation of slides, team collaboration and content management to the analysis and output of presentations.

FOUNDING STORY

Martin was project manager at a digital agency, Hannes was his client and is now in the role of head of marketing, and Martin L. was a web developer at the agency. The idea came directly from problems experienced in the role of head of marketing or international product manager.

FINANCING

Until now, we have been financed by our own funds, a two-year Austrian Research Promotion Agency (FFG) Basisprogramm grant, two business angel investment rounds, a double equity loan and our generated revenue. Some of our customers are corporations, but we have no corporate partners.

MARKET REACH

We currently focus on the DACH region, but our customers use presono worldwide. Our next markets will be across Europe, then the United States and Asia.

WHY AUSTRIA?

We could count on a business network to address first companies and get feedback about our idea, and we had dynamic knowledge of the target market in Austria.

In Austria, there would be an improved startup success rate with more possibilities to fail without risks over personal bankruptcy and a US-like mindset to invest in ideas and think big about the future, and instead of just looking at current revenues.

LEARNING

If we could start over, we would get a higher investment earlier and/or not expand the team (and increase costs) that fast. We have learned that increasing the number of team members can lead to more work and challenges, and that sometimes it is too early for your technology or idea to be accepted by the larger part of the market.

COVID-19

We have been negatively affected by the crisis due to the fact that most of our target companies have reduced working hours and have halted investments until the end of the year. We have been on hold in most cases, even if the companies have a need for our solution. We have adapted our development roadmap to push features that support collaboration from home office as well as sales presentations done via web sessions.

presono.com

SUPPORTED BY

go international

Federal Ministry Republic of Austria Digital and Economic Affairs

WKO

GRAZI

STORYCLASH

A social media monitoring tool for leading international brands, offering a real-time view of what's trending via social media interactions

FOUNDED	EXPECTED EXIT	INVESTMENT	HQ	SECTOR	EMPLOYEES
2015	1-100 YEARS (MERGER, TRADE/SALE, IPO)	2 MILLION	LINZ	MARTECH	25

FOUNDERS
Andreas Gutzelnig, Philip Penner

BIO
Social media teams use Storyclash to measure, optimize and communicate the value of their social media campaigns and influencers, benchmark themselves against the industry and discover new content trends. With Storyclash, brands, publishers and agencies are able to discover viral content, watch competitors in real-time and make data-driven decisions to get more website traffic and higher engagement.

FOUNDING STORY
The founders met at the Institute for Higher Education Perg and the Vienna University of Technology. The idea came out of our previous work at a media company. We wanted to make data-driven decisions based on social media data.

FINANCING
The company is financed by grants and investors. We are taking the venture capital growth route.

MARKET REACH
We are active in the DACH region and in EU countries, including Italy, the Netherlands, Denmark, Sweden and Hungary. Our next step will be rolling out across the EU.

WHY AUSTRIA?
Austria was the best choice for founding due to the grants and subsidies ecosystem, alongside a high-quality education system. One possibility for Austria to improve its startup ecosystem would be a government matching fund for startup investment.

LEARNING
We would have raised more money and invested it all in the product. Having learned so much in the past five years since founding, every day is better than the last.

COVID-19
We did not change our business model and were not really affected by the COVID-19 outbreak, as social media monitoring is more important than before.

storyclash.com

“There are subsidies for nearly every phase of a startup, which support newcomers not only with money but also with know-how.”

SYMFLOWER

Let machines test your software autonomously – 1,000 times faster and 100 times more accurate than a human tester

FOUNDED	EXPECTED EXIT	INVESTMENT	HQ	SECTOR	EMPLOYEES
2018	5 YEARS (TRADE/SALE, IPO)	1.5 MILLION	LINZ	SOFTWARE TESTING	13

FOUNDERS

Evelyn Haslinger, Markus Zimmermann

BIO

Symflower employs artificial intelligence and mathematical models to test your software. It generates test cases 1000 times faster and 100 times more accurate than writing them manually.
Symflower is able to automatically find bugs and security issues in source code, without a human being having to do anything.
With their product they abruptly increase the productivity of software developers up to 40 percent and simultaneously raise the quality of software products to an unprecedented level.

FOUNDING STORY

They met each other at the university during their studies. Markus had the idea to build a product capable of testing software without human intervention. In 2015, Markus asked Evelyn if she wanted to help him to build a software prototype in their leisure time. She agreed and both started to work on the worldwide first autonomous software testing product, based on AI and mathematical models.

FINANCING

We have received various public subsidies (FFG, AWS and others), investments from our three managing directors and investment from eQventure as well as a running business with turnover. In total we've raised € 1.5 million, within 12 months.

MARKET REACH

We are active worldwide helping clients to fully automatically detect bugs, performance problems and security issues in their source code. We are selling ourr products directly as well as indirectly via resellers to their clientsl. More and more companies worldwide are starting to become a reseller for our products.

WHY AUSTRIA?

We need highly educated people in our company to be able to further develop our technology. At Symflower we are not only writing code, but also heavily involved in basic research. Austria has the advantage of good universities and professors, both lead to well educated people that fit our requirements and also attract massive talent to Austria. Austria is an excellent place for founders. There are subsidies for nearly every phase of a startup, which support newcomers not only with money but also with know-how. It would certainly help if the knowledge about existing subsidies was better spread.

LEARNING

We would start from the beginning as a limited company (GmbH), because it has cost us unnecessary extra money and time to change our company type. It was very difficult for us to find new employees at the beginning. Many candidates were put off at the start by Symflower since we were so small and had no investors on board. We ended up hiring people who, as we found out later, unfortunately did not always fit into the team and we had to part with some of them. Today, it is much easier for us to find new employees. We have learned to pay much more attention to the skills of the candidates during the job interviews than at the beginning of our company. We also pay more attention to whether candidates really fit into our team in terms of their personality.

COVID-19

Symflower's mission is to liberate people from the burden of software testing. This has not changed since our company was founded. COVID-19 had no negative impact on business.

symflower.com

SUPPORTED BY

go international

Federal Ministry Republic of Austria Digital and Economic Affairs

WKO

"For us, entrepreneurship does not mean to 'have an idea' so much as it is important to listen to customers at the right time."

SYMVARO

Developing mobile applications to help water and waste utilities to adapt to the digital age thanks to a simple, smart and efficient solution

FOUNDED	EXPECTED EXIT	INVESTMENT	HQ	SECTOR	EMPLOYEES
2010	MERGER, TRADE/SALE, IPO	>2 MILLION	KLAGENFURT	WATER	25

FOUNDERS

Rudolf Ball, Philip Kozeny

BIO

The company provides software as a service (SaaS) for water and waste comanies to digitize their processes and connect with their citizens. This makes work easier, plannable and reduces problems. Symvaro makes it easier for regions, cities, municipalities and their utilities to become smarter - through simple, easily integrated solutions with high added value for city administrations and citizens.

FOUNDING STORY

For us entrepreneurship does not mean to "have an idea" so much as it is important to listen to customers at the right time. So, when we created our products, the ideas came from our customers, and together we brought them the all way to a successful product.

FINANCING

The company was initially bootstrap financed, then through business angels and after that, venture capital.
We have large, strategic investment from a corporation, and we try to divide investment and cooperation as much as possible. The hardest part is to develop common success stories where both parts can play their strengths and both parts win. We believe a startup-corporate cooperation is a long game and that it takes a lot of trust and willpower to take the ride. Finally, both can win and both can learn a lot from the other side.

MARKET REACH

Today we are active in Austria and Germany, but in 2021, we will take the step into two or three new countries together with sales and implementation partners.

WHY AUSTRIA?

Austria has been a great choice because of its stability in nearly every aspect of life: government, finance, utilities. We believe that success is a mindset game, so in order to change the mindset of future entrepreneurs - more risk, more sales, more passion - entrepreneurial studies in the education system would be needed - the earlier, the better (at university is too late).

LEARNING

If we could start over, we would find paying customers first, find a sales channel, and only after that, start developing the product or service. Our greatest challenge so far has been the transformation of the role of a founder or CEO and what it means to work on - not in - the company. We describe it as a journey that needs a lot of trust, control and a complete change of responsibilities - hard, but worth it.

COVID-19

We have been affected positively by the crisis. We adapted our products in various steps to secure a safe distance between our customers and our clients' customers. We offered a module for distance reading of water meters for free to all customers. Approximately half of them took that offer. We have developed two new products, which empower water companies to work in a world with social distancing. We think every crisis can become an opportunity, too, but you have to want it to be one.

symvaro.com

“We wish for a more positive perception of entrepreneurship and easier access to venture capital.”

TUBICS

A software-as-a-service platform that supports companies to amplify their branded content on YouTube

FOUNDED	EXPECTED EXIT	INVESTMENT	HQ	SECTOR	EMPLOYEES
2017	TRADE/SALE	1 MILLION	VIENNA	AI	10

FOUNDERS
Claudia Eder, Matthias Funk, Matthias Posch

BIO
tubics gives you data-driven ideas for YouTube videos that get you views and brand awareness in your niche. Every video idea includes search volume, trend, competitor insights, questions to cover in the video, and suggested metadata. Our YouTube SEO software supports thousands of channel managers to grow their channels via Search and Discovery and has already over 20.000 connected YouTube channels.

FOUNDING STORY
Matthias and Claudia worked together in a video marketing agency before founding tubics. While consulting our clients, we found out that most companies lack knowhow and data regarding YouTube. In order to gather more data for our consulting projects we used a prototype that later became the tubics platform.

FINANCING
The company is financed by a combination of angel money, grants and revenues. We work with corporations in innovation projects and will soon launch a major sales partnership.

MARKET REACH
We are a company with a global offering. The majority of our enterprise customers come from the DACH region (Germany, Austria, Switzerland) but we are currently expanding to other countries as well.

WHY AUSTRIA?
We enjoy being based in Austria because it is small and easy to network, for its availability of public grants and great living quality with affordable housing, and therefore affordable staff. We wish for a more positive perception of entrepreneurship in general, lower taxes on wages and earnings, less bureaucracy and easier access to venture capital.

LEARNING
Starting over, we would build a strong and experienced management team early on and be even clearer about the company and product vision. Our biggest challenges and lessons learned revolved around getting distracted with side projects and not focus on our core product value enough.

COVID-19
Our vision and product remained the same, but we adapted sales strategies and pricing. We were negatively affected at the beginning of the COVID-19 crisis because of budget cuts in many enterprises and postponed projects, but the effects where small and not long term.

SUPPORTED BY

go international

Federal Ministry Republic of Austria Digital and Economic Affairs

WKO

tubics.com

"We would never ever make our business model dependent on a third party like Facebook again."

XALEON

An engagement software that supports organizations in seamless and friction-free digital engagement and interaction with their customers

FOUNDED	EXPECTED EXIT	INVESTMENT	HQ	SECTOR	EMPLOYEES
2018	MERGER, IPO	<1 MILLION	LINZ	FINTECH, INSURTECH, SAAS	20

FOUNDERS

Horst-Georg Fuchs, Mathias Holzinger, Markus Wagner

BIO

Xaleon (formerly Chatvisor) provides engagement software that supports organisations in seamless and friction-free digital engagement and interaction with their customers. Xaleon's Engagement Platform enables clients to empower their sales, customer services and marketing teams to mirror in-person experiences, enabling them to remain competitive in a world of hyperconnectivity and personalisation.

FOUNDING STORY

To discover what Xaleon refers to as one of our core technologies today, we needed a meeting with a well-known German car brand. While the course of the meeting itself cannot be considered as ideal, the lunch and ongoing conversation with our contact person afterward unveiled that there is a problem to be solved. That got us started developing our leading co-browsing technology. Today, the technological core of co-browsing is both foundation and influencer of features across Xaleon's whole platform.

FINANCING

Xaleon generated revenue from day one and was able to cover a decent amount of its monthly burn through its early revenue. In addition, Xaleon has been successful in obtaining external financing through grants and other public funding from the Austrian Research Promotion Agency (FFG), Austria Wirtschaftsservice (AWS), tech2b and Upper Austrian Credit Guarantee Society (OÖ.UBG). Further, Xaleon received an investment from Austrian venture capitalist eQventure.

MARKET REACH

In 2020, Xaleon set its focus on its home market, the DACH region. Next, Xaleon will expand to other markets such as BeNeLux and UK. By entering and positioning Xaleon in the UK market, the company plans to gain a foothold in the Anglo-Saxon market, and from there also enter other markets such as the Nordics.

WHY AUSTRIA?

Austria is a great country to found a company for many reasons. Xaleon is happy to be based in a country that produces good talent and has a reasonable balance between living costs and salaries. As a young founding team without private capital to finance our startup, we appreciate and want to outline the offering and opportunities provided by the Austrian government, which helped us tremendously along our journey. If there are two things to improve, it is that there could always be more talent available, and that there could be a better exchange between successful entrepreneurs and young founders.

LEARNING

Firstly, Xaleon would never ever make our business model dependent on a third party like Facebook again. Secondly, the Xaleon team would invest more time at the beginning of the startup journey to properly discover, discuss and understand the problems in the respective target industries.

COVID-19

For Xaleon it was both good and bad at the same time. On one hand, Xaleon had to postpone and even lose promising deals that were already at a later stage through budget cuts and reduction of workforce; on the other hand, we are experiencing an increased interest toward speeding up digitalization in certain industries.

xaleon.com

SUPPORTED BY

go international

Federal Ministry Republic of Austria Digital and Economic Affairs

WKO AUSSENWIRTSCHAFT AUSTRIA

YODEL.IO

Make your phone calls simpler, easier to handle and more collaborative - and all this in Slack

FOUNDED	EXPECTED EXIT	INVESTMENT	HQ	SECTOR	EMPLOYEES
2016	3 YEARS (TRADE/SALE)	2.3 MILLION	VIENNA	BUSINESS SOFTWARE/SAAS	6

FOUNDERS

David Heininger, Mike Heininger, Nina Hoedlmayr, Mario Uher

BIO

Yodel is a phone system that joins customer service teams team as a receptionist. It prequalifies inbound voice communications and allows call management without switching tools.

FOUNDING STORY

The idea came as a necessity for us - we are, by design, a remote team and hated being interrupted by phone calls. Thus, we built a product that was the solution to our own problems.

FINANCING

Yodel was originally bootstrapped by the founders, but rather quickly received the first investments from early-stage funds and business angels. We have initiated several partnerships with corporates in Austria and abroad. However, these experiences were rather unsuccessful, either because the other side took too long in its decision processes or by not properly executing the agreed-upon activities. As a startup, we believe that you cannot afford the time or heavy resources without quick wins, thus ending partnerships quicker is necessary. However, we also experienced successful agreements. The underlying factor is agreeing upon smaller milestones that are easier to reach and moving forward step by step.

MARKET REACH

Yodel is present throughout the world, but our major target market is the United States, where we are further investing to compete with other players.

WHY AUSTRIA?

The main benefit of being based in Austria is the public infrastructure of support for young and innovative companies - this ranges from direct grants to indirect initiatives like Go Silicon Valley. However, we wish for less bureaucracy and fewer taxes to improve the ecosystem.

LEARNING

The most important lessons from founding our company are the following: focus and stick with one very concrete niche, build the best product for this one target group, and only then expand to other fields.

COVID-19

Although some businesses needed to cancel their Yodel subscription to keep costs low during COVID-19, most businesses actually needed to rely more on their phones, especially in light of needing a phone system that is reliable for remote teams. In this context, Yodel has been positively influenced, as more businesses signed up to use Yodel during the crisis.

yodel.io

SUPPORTED BY

go international

Federal Ministry Republic of Austria Digital and Economic Affairs

WKO

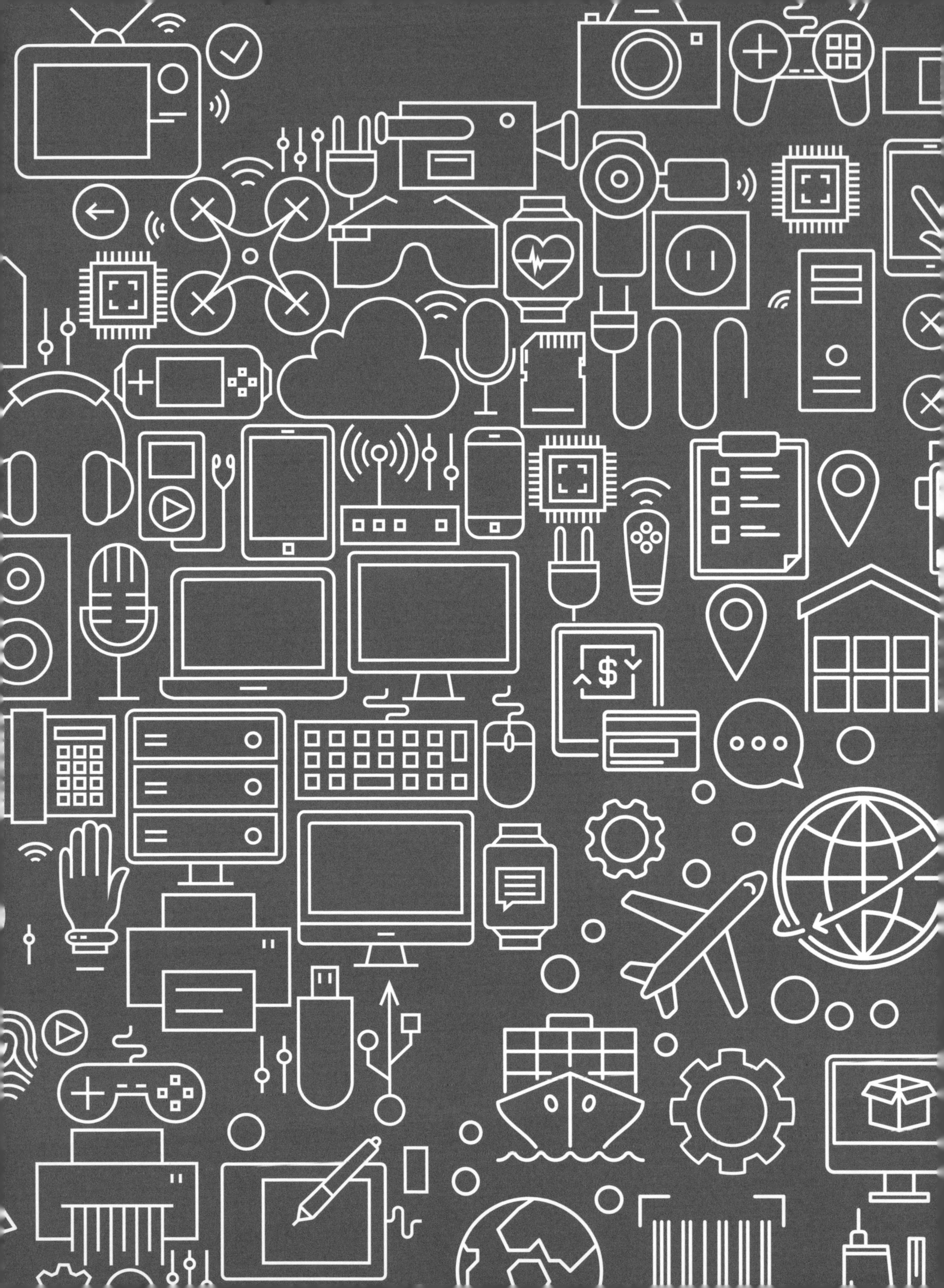

About 100 STARTUPS MADE IN AUSTRIA

W48
STARTUP LOFTS
SATURO
nativy

ABOUT 100 STARTUPS MADE IN AUSTRIA

BACKGROUND

The idea for *100 Startups Made in Austria* was developed together with the publishing house Home Town Media. The aim of the book is to generate more international attention to the rising startup ecosystem in Austria. The new book is based on the approximately 6-year-old book project *Erfolgsgründer – Made in Austria* (Fabian Greiler, Helmut Pöllinger and Berthold Baurek-Karlic). However, it will be an evolution. This time, the community itself will decide who will be invited for an interview in the book.

WHY 100 STARTUPS – MADE IN AUSTRIA?

Austria's startup ecosystem has emerged as a global player over the past decade. The chance to change the world and make it a better, smarter or more sustainable place drives founders and their stories. According to the Austrian Startup Monitor 2019, also published by Home Town Media, more than 2,200 startups have been founded in Austria since 2008. Startups factor into the economy significantly, as 9 out of 10 startups plan to hire employees in the next 12 months. That's a growth rate of around 40%. At the end of 2019, roughly 17,500 people were working in Austrian startups, a full 52% of the companies were financed with external growth capital and 90% generates revenues abroad. This is the DNA of a next generation of hidden champions. TechCrunch recently called Austria an emerging startup hub, due to its maturing investors and founders, and the availability of government support schemes.

METHOD

The startups represented in the book were voted on by the public. They were asked to vote on which startups they love and deserve to be showcased most. The book highlights the 10 most prominent sectors, from Health Tech to FinTech and artificial intelligence. The variety of prominent startups suggests the breadth of Austria's startup ingenuity, attractiveness and availability of talent, made possible by the high-quality education in Austria and incentive structures supported by government initiatives.

The selected startups were asked to fill out a survey, answering questions about their founding experience, why it was beneficial to found in Austria and the impacts of COVID-19. This book represents not only their successes and capacity to corner niche industries, but also their resilience and capacity to adapt to challenges like COVID-19.

HOMETOWN MEDIA

VENIONAIRE CAPITAL

Venionaire Capital is an entrepreneurial partner for investors, founders, and institutions. Their partners and team are specialized in venture capital and private equity investments, with an extensive track record over more than a decade. They offer transaction and corporate advisory services – from due diligence, valuation, deal structuring, and (ghost) negotiating to alternative fund management – for investors, corporates, public entities, and growth companies, including startups and scaleups. Their track record as entrepreneurs, advisers and investors is represented in the total volume of deals reaching over €1 billion, for corporate finance, venture capital, corporate startup engagement, digital transformation, and high-tech innovation. They also serve as trusted partners for scouting, screening, technology-, market- and competitive-analysis and valuation for bespoke investors and accelerators in Europe.

Venionaire Captial offers services for investors, founders, and institutions:

MERGERS & ACQUISITIONS

They offer guidance and advisory on merging, buying and selling businesses, especially due to the high cost and loss associated with mistakes. There are increasing numbers of stakeholders involved in transactions, such as tax advisors, lawyers, technology, and other experts, creating more complexity than ever in transaction management. Their team of specialists will work with clients until they cross the finish line and beyond.

FUND SERVICES

Venionaire Capital provides fund setup and documentation; fund strategy, in which they develop portfolio strategies and business plans; deal sourcing and services, where they provide a high-quality deal flow through active scouting; cooperations with partners; and fund administration in which they manage all aspects of a fund's administration.

VALUATION

Valuing companies, scaleups or startups for investors is as much an art as it is a science: Risk factors reflect high levels of uncertainty, multiples are based on comparable transactions and applied models take exits into account. Additional parameters such as dilution through future rounds, availability of critical data of multiples and more make venture valuations significantly more difficult than valuing mature companies.

CORPORATE STARTUPS ENGAGEMENT

Corporate Startup engagement (CSE) arrived in Europe and has evolved into a key aspect of corporate strategy to remain future-proof in a digitalized world. Corporates have begun experimenting with startup programs. Startup challenges have become a new normal across industries, generating a budding interest in ideas, talents, services, or products that can speed up innovation significantly with insights from today's investment and startup environment.

90% SUCCESS RATE FOR TRANSACTIONS

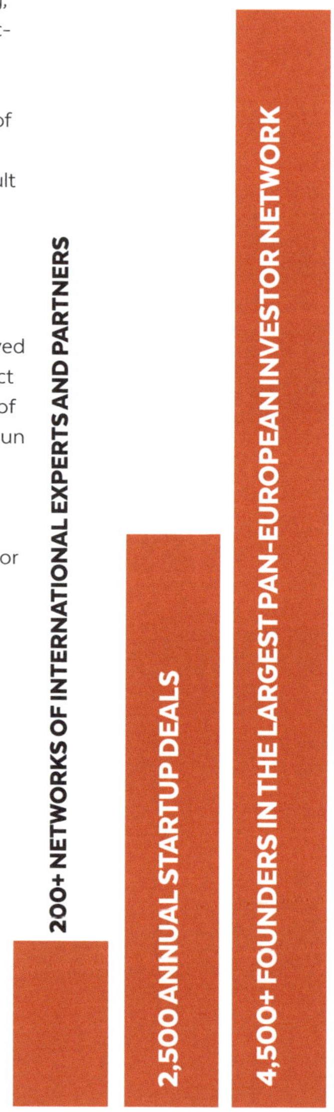

EUROPEAN SUPER ANGELS CLUB

The European Super Angels Club (ESAC) is a Pan-European co-investment and networking club for super business angels, high-net-worth individuals, family offices, venture capital firms, and corporate innovation units. Their members combine their individual financial strength and know-how to invest in high-growth European startups.

The club offers its members access to international co-investments and a pro-active fund-management for syndicated super angels investments. Selected business cases are presented at recurring "Invest and Connect" roadshows throughout Europe, after being scouted and analyzed by a global team of experts. In 2017, the initiative was founded by Partners of KPMG Austria and Venionaire Capital.

ESAC provides an investment platform for highly scalable European companies, with services for investors and for entrepreneurs:

FOR INVESTORS

CHOICE

- Access top European tech deals, increasing your deal flow
- Create your own portfolio by investing in their pre-screened deals
- Choose your own deals and nominate startups to join the platform

CLARITY

- ESAC supports you from initial interest to investment completion
- All information about each startup is available 24/7 through ESAC's online investment portal
- You benefit from startup due diligence and investment analysis by KPMG and Venionaire Capital

EXPERTISE

- A seamless onboarding experience and support
- Use of tax-efficient, special-purpose vehicles
- Risk diversification across the portfolio
- Quarterly reports on your investments
- Proactive search for exit opportunities and returns

FOR ENTREPRENEURS

WINGS

- ESAC is your friend, colleague and partner on your entrepreneurial journey. They are there for you through the ups, downs and all the way to exit.

FINANCE

- They finance companies they believe are ready to scale across Europe and beyond and specifically look for.
- Highly qualified and committed teams
- Traction within your domestic market and high potential for scalability
- High exit probability

OPEN DOORS

- Through their combined network of partners and associations, they open doors at some of Europe's top companies to help you win the key contracts and further financing to scale your business.
- Their team is made up of financial and professional services specialists, entrepreneurs and tech experts.
- Rooted in central Europe, they aim to finance the growth of tomorrow's European tech giants.

AUTHORS

FLORIAN KANDLER

is one of Austria's most well-known startup coaches. In addition to his consulting activities with a focus on investor search, pitching and sales, he operates and supports targeted initiatives for knowledge exchange, aimed at young entrepreneurs – This book is just such an initiative. The successful founders of the 100 startups in this book share valuable knowledge and helpful insights that help the next generation of founders.
In the past he's launched projects for young entrpreneurs like the *Startup Report* **(StartupReport.at)**, which has been published annually since 2016, his podcasts *Startup Milestones* **(StartupMilestones.eu)** and *Gründer & Zünder* **(DerStartupPodcast.com)**.
Florian also teaches and gives consulting in workshops and as a lecturer at numerous accelerators, incubators, universities, technical colleges and educational institutions. He has also boiled down insights for founders into his book as an author (*Business Angels/Devils*, **BusinessAngelBuch.at**). He is the official pitch coach for the TV show *2 Minutes 2 Million* (Austria's answer to *Shark Tank*), the innovation conferences Fifteen Seconds and 4Gamechangers, the Vienna Business Agency and the #glaubandich Challenge.
He continues to share his knowledge online with founders throughout Europe, with useful tips and strategies for the successful investor search for in English at **GetFunding.how**. At **DerPerfektePitch.com** he reveals some of his most successful pitch methods, tested on investors in Silicon Valley, London, Berlin and Vienna. Two of the companies he co-founded and built up in a management capacity have been able to attract over three million euros from venture capital firms and business angels from the United States and Europe.
FlorianKandler.com

At the beginning of 2020, we came up with idea for *100 Startups Made in Austria*. Over the course of the COVID-19 pandemic, many startups from Austria struggled with lockdowns and travel bans. Coming from a small country with world-class companies and products, the need for international markets is nothing new. The pandemic made it apparent, however, that startups from the Alpine Republic would have to internationalize more quickly than companies from larger European neighbors like Germany or France. With this book we hope to help spread the word about Austria's 100 best startups. Our partnership with Advantage Austria and go.international give us a truly international audience of business-oriented global citizens.

Austria produces great startups, but the spring board here is limited. To achieve something that truly disrupts or improves an industry, future European tech giants have to think of the international markets up-front.

There is great potential on the continent, and we are convinced that Austria, in particular, has a bright future in tech. We were stumped when selecting which startups would be included in the 100 Startups. Being data-driven people, we decided to let the crowd decide – specifically the Austrian startup community. The voting campaign had a immense

BERTHOLD BAUREK-KARLIC

is a serial founder and managing director of Venionaire Capital, a group specializing in M&A and venture capital, which includes the syndicate fund, European Super Angels Club (EXF Alpha), the investment company Motec Ventures (**motec.vc**) and the software provider Dealmatrix (**dealmatrix.com**). He is also Secretary General of the Business Angel Institute (**businessangelinstitute.org**), President of the European Super Angels Club (**superangels.club**), Expert Partner of various accelerators and advisor to various venture funds. As a blogger, author and board member of the Austrian Private Equity and Venture Capital Association (**avco.at**), he actively promotes the startup ecosystem in Austria.
baurek-karlic.at

impact. The competition to make the list was tough, so congratulations to the winners.

We believe that Austria is a great location, both for startups and innovative thinkers. With this book, we aim to promote the hidden champions of the future. Effectively, it's also a step to take them out of hiding, because, as you will see, some are already champions.

In a perfect world, the availability of venture capital would correspond with the quality of the companies they help scale – we regularly observe new funds and business angels emerging and we hope to help them connect and collaborate better with international stars of the investor scene.

Austria's talents have what it takes, we've proven that time and again. Our founders get out of the regional comfort zone early and that is a real asset when building resilient, crisis-proof companies. When we as venture capital investors think about the international success stories of the future, we are not only looking for the best business models, services and technologies – we are looking for strong teams that can make a venture a global success.

In the pages of this book, you'll see 100 of teams that can do just that. We hope you enjoy their inspirational stories. You could be part of their next step to greatness.

INDEX